COACH
Parenting

Raising Teenagers *with* Advice *from*

Pro Football's Greatest Head Coaches

ERIKA KATZ

D0066845

RIVER GROVE
BOOKS

This book is intended as a reference volume only. It is sold with the understanding that the publisher and author are not engaged in rendering any professional services. The information given here is designed to help you make informed decisions. If you suspect that you have a problem that might require professional treatment or advice, you should seek competent help.

Published by River Grove Books
Austin, TX
www.rivergrovebooks.com

Distributed by River Grove Books

Design and composition by Greenleaf Book Group
Cover design by Greenleaf Book Group
Cover images by Mliberra and Billion Photos. Copyright ©2017.
Used under license from Shutterstock.com
Whistle icon made by Yannick from www.flaticon.com; Football, goal, megaphone, helmet, lasagna icons made by Freepik from www.flaticon.com

Cataloging-in-Publication data is available.

Print ISBN: 978-1-63299-143-0

eBook ISBN: 978-1-63299-144-7

First Edition

This book is dedicated to
my son, Stone, and my daughter, Somer.

I know as your mother I am supposed to be the teacher and the coach. But I learn so much from both of you every day. Stone, thank you for teaching me about football and being so supportive of this book. Somer, thank you for your energy and your encouragement as I embarked on this journey. You both inspire everything I do, and I am forever grateful to have such loving, kind, and supportive children. I love you both with all of my heart.

CONTENTS

FOREWORD

I n 1992, I was thirty-six years old and landed a job as quarterbacks coach of the Green Bay Packers. My wife, Gayle, and I were a young couple and excited for this new adventure. Soon after I arrived in Green Bay, General Manager Ron Wolf asked me to evaluate a young quarterback playing for Atlanta named Brett Favre. Although he was a third-string quarterback and not playing much, we saw something in him and decided to trade our number one draft pick for Brett. Our trade would change the Green Bay Packers and my coaching life forever.

Brett was a talented young player, but as green as it gets. I figured he could spend his first season learning from our veteran starting quarterback, Don Majkowski. But in football, like in life, you have to be ready for anything! It was September, and we were playing the Cincinnati Bengals. Early in the game, Majkowski tore up his ankle and was taken off the field. Enter Brett Favre.

Brett did everything imaginable. He fumbled, threw interceptions, made spectacular throws, improvised on the fly, and did things I never coached him to do. With just thirteen seconds left on the clock, he threw a game-tying touchdown pass and the crowd went nuts. He jumped around like a kid, showing that emotion we would later come to see from Brett. He even ran off the field to the bench and took off his helmet, *forgetting* that he had to hold for the extra point to win the game. I was up in the press box and had to get Brett back out on the field so we could get the extra point for the win!

I quickly realized if I was going to coach Brett, I had to look out for him, protect him, and hold him accountable just like a father would do for his child. Although I loved laughing and having fun with him, he had to see me as an authority figure if I wanted to get him to play to his potential. That's when I learned what being a coach really meant—doing what's best for my quarterback even if he wasn't always happy about it. When Brett was late for one of my quarterback meetings, as bad as I felt about doing it, I fined him $200 (which was a lot for him back then). I had to set a standard. It was the last time he was ever late.

In 1997, I became the head coach of the San Francisco 49ers and had the opportunity to coach legends such as Steve Young and Jerry Rice. Steve and Jerry were already Super Bowl champions and Pro Bowlers. I didn't have to start from scratch like with Brett. But, I did have to exude confidence and capability to earn their trust and respect. If coaching Brett was like parenting a toddler, coaching Steve and Jerry was more like parenting young adults—the dynamics were different, but the responsibilities equally important.

As my children became teenagers, my coaching skills came in handy. There are many similarities between coaching a football team and parenting your children. Whether it's your players or your kids, you have to be present, take an interest in their personal life, and lead them by being a good role model. Most importantly, whether it's coaching or parenting, you have to have a game plan and stay true to your core set of values.

When Erika reached out to me about the idea of parenting like a coach, it really resonated. I thought about my own experiences with my dad, who was a wrestling coach. When I was graduating from high school, he wrote an anonymous letter that was published in the *Iron Mountain News*, our local town paper in Michigan. The letter was titled "Open Letter from Father to Son."

In that letter, he wrote what he valued most in me. It was not how many points I scored in a game or whether I was MVP, but the way I conducted myself. He wrote, "I've learned from you, son—about loyalty, and fair play, and I admire your optimism and your philosophy of life." His proudest moment was when a coach said to him, "He's the kind of son I would like to have!" To my dad, coaching and parenting were not just about winning, but about being a person of character.

As both a former NFL head coach and a father of four grown children, I have brought coaching into my parenting and parenting into my coaching. A successful coach, like a devoted parent, is a great teacher and uses a combination of love and discipline to help their players and their children realize their potential and become champions in life.

Steve Mariucci
"Coach Mooch"

ACKNOWLEDGMENTS

When I first had the idea for this book, I never dreamed I would get to speak to Super Bowl–winning coaches, Pro Football Hall of Fame players, and legendary broadcasters. Then I was introduced to Bob Costas, who shared his intelligence and wisdom with me. His encouragement was truly a gift, and this book would not have taken form without him.

Steve Mariucci, thank you for teaching me how to draw a legal football formation and for sharing your stories about your football career and your family life. Your short film *Father Figures* is a testament to how coaching and parenting really are one and the same.

Troy Aikman, I loved learning about your football experiences and all the life lessons that came with it. Howie Long, your commitment to your sons, your community, and the game of football is an inspiration to us all. Jimmy Johnson, you have inspired me to expect the best of myself and my children each day. Thank you to Tom Coughlin for showing by example how to parent with strength and inspire a future generation to give back to the world.

Lawrence Tynes, I am grateful for your help and for teaching me to be at my best when it counts the most.

John Harbaugh, your exuberance and energy made me feel like anything is possible, and every day I think of *What's Important Now!* Jim Harbaugh, you taught me how to be a teacher to my children, and now—to parents everywhere. Brian Billick, you inspired me to not just be a mother to my children but to also be their role model. Dave Wannstedt, your commitment to family and faith helped me bring those values into my home.

Barry Switzer, I love your stories, your sense of humor, and the fact that you always "do what you say you're gonna do!" Mike Shanahan, you taught me about preparation in both football and the field of life.

Dick Vermeil, from you I learned that while caring is the best part of parenting, it's also sometimes the hardest. Mike Zimmer, you made me understand how just putting an arm around your child and speaking to them kindly can be all they need to make a change.

Tiki Barber, I enjoyed learning the many ways you can teach the same lesson. Thank you to Jedd Fisch for sharing your thoughts on coaching both college and pro athletes. To my Dartmouth family—Jay Fiedler, Buddy Teevens, and Steve Lewinstein—thank you for your Big Green support and your belief in me and this book.

Dr. Mark Unterberg, your vast knowledge of sports psychology and what makes a great coach gave me a whole new perspective. James Dunning Jr., your dedication to making the sports experience better for young players has transformed the lives of many young athletes.

Thank you to Marlene and Eddie Landau and Alan and Linda Landis for helping with my first interview. Your belief in me meant so much, and I am grateful for your support. Jerry and Donna Slipakoff, you were there from day one cheering me on. Thank you for believing in my project and introducing me to Coach Vermeil.

Thank you to Lyss Stern for telling me I could do this every single day! Rafael, your excitement to read my unedited notes gave me the encouragement I needed to power through draft after draft. To Amy Rosenblum and Drew Auer, thank you for your excitement and passion for *Coach Parenting*.

And finally, thanks to my mom, who is my biggest cheerleader; to my dad, who taught me how to be a writer and encouraged me to keep writing; and to my brother, whose humor got me through many a writer's block. Thank you to my husband, Jay, for your love, support, and encouragement every step of the way, and for watching every episode of *A Football Life* and *Hard Knocks* with me, embracing coach parenting in our home, and teaching me about football. Thank you to my children, Stone and Somer, for making me so proud each and every day to be your mom. You are my championship team!

THE PREGAME—START PARENTING LIKE A COACH

My son had just turned fourteen. I walked into the den and saw a pair of sneakers on the floor at the foot of the couch. I said, "Honey, before you go out, can you please put your shoes in your closet?" (His room is about ten feet from the den, so I was not asking him to climb stairs or exert himself.) A day later, I asked again, "Sweetie, will you please put your shoes in your closet?" Another day went by, and those smelly sneakers were still there! I marched into his room and sternly said, "If your sneakers are not picked up in five minutes, I am throwing them in the garbage."

He looked at me in disbelief and said, "Fine." At a snail's pace, he picked up his shoes and tossed them into his room. Not exactly the "Yes, Mom, I'll put them neatly in the closet" that I had hoped for.

A week later, after the second half of his varsity basketball game, his coach asked him to pick up his sneakers, the sneakers of four other players, some cones, and three balls. My son's response? "Yes, Coach. I'm on it."

I turned to the coach and said, "How did you do that? It takes me three days to get him to pick up one pair of sneakers!"

His coach laughed and said, "You just gotta be firm from the get-go and let him know you mean business." At that moment, it dawned on me. I had to *stop* parenting like a mom and *start* parenting like a coach!

That night, I scrolled through Amazon to find books written by successful coaches. I came across *The Score Takes Care of Itself* by Bill Walsh, the late head coach of the San Francisco 49ers. I thought, *If he could coach football greats like Joe Montana, maybe he could teach me something about coaching my teenagers.* I ordered the book and found it was chock-full of ideas on how to be a better communicator and motivate players to be their best. It inspired me to delve deeper into the world of football coaching. After all, *football can't be played alone. It's the ultimate team sport, and it requires discipline, sacrifice, love, and teamwork—all the elements of a successful family.*

My son is a huge Giants fan, so my next book was *Earn the Right to Win* by former New York Giants head coach Tom Coughlin. Then, I found a book from the 1990s—*Turn the Thing Around*—by former Dallas Cowboys head coach Jimmy Johnson. Next, it was *Win Forever* by the Seattle Seahawks head coach Pete Carroll.

I watched every episode of *A Football Life* on the NFL Network and took notes! I found a brilliant commencement speech on YouTube given by Baltimore Ravens head coach John Harbaugh. Then, I binge-watched *All or Nothing: A Season with the Arizona Cardinals* on Amazon Prime. As I watched head coach Bruce Arians work with his team throughout the entire season, I was completely mesmerized. While Sunday nights used to be dedicated to *Real Housewives*, now it was all about *Sunday Night Football*!

By then, my son had turned fifteen and my daughter was thirteen. At this point, I was completely obsessed with football coaching, and it was time to apply what I had learned. I started with a simple rule common to every football organization: BE ON TIME!

My kids have cell phones and always call me when they're going to be late. Often, I end up excusing tardiness because I know where they are. That was until my son started going out with friends on Saturday nights. I gave him an 11:00 p.m. curfew. But then, he'd be out with friends and start calling me at 10:50 saying he was having trouble getting a cab, or he was having fun, and asking if he could come home at 11:30. Most of the time, I would say yes, because I knew he was safe and he *had* called to ask if it was okay. But each week, his ETA kept getting later and later. I had set curfew at 11:00, but he was finessing 11:30 and even 11:45.

One Saturday night, I decided to change the game on him. Before he went out, I said, "Your curfew is 11:00 p.m. tonight. If you're late, it will be earlier next Saturday night, and I'm adding a five-minute penalty for every five minutes you come in after eleven."

I may as well have said it to the wall, because at 10:50 I got the call to ask for more time. To his surprise, I said no. By then, he was running late, assuming I would cave as I had in the past. When he walked in at 11:10, I told him next week he had to be home at 10:40—which was ten minutes earlier than normal, with a ten-minute penalty incurred for being late.

Like all the great head coaches, I followed through on the consequence I set for breaking a rule. After a few weeks, he started coming home five minutes early to show me he was listening. In just three months, punctuality became part of his daily life. He was completing his assignments in school in advance and as a result, improved his grades. He was even being more helpful around the house. Everything improved from just implementing *one* rule.

That's when I realized I was on to something.

With no personal connections to football, I set out to interview as many superstar head football coaches as would talk to me. I wanted to learn how I could parent my teenagers the same way they coached their players.

These were my goals:

- Build character in my kids

- Motivate them to be their best

- Be consistent in my dealings with them

- Hold them accountable for their actions

- Command their respect

With an idea and a dream, I emailed NFL football teams to request interviews with players and coaches. I went to college with Jay Fiedler, who played in the NFL for ten years and was the starting quarterback for the Miami Dolphins. After a bit of Googling, I discovered he and his brother Scott own and run the highly regarded Sports Academy at Brookwood Camps in Glen Spey, New York, an overnight camp where Jay coaches and mentors kids each summer. He also runs Prime Time Sports Camps, a year-round football training program. I emailed him, and he was excited to help me. His dad was a championship high school basketball coach in New York City and brought many of his coaching skills into parenting Jay and his brother:

> "My dad was the best coach I ever knew. His two phrases were 'The cream always rises to the top' and 'Big players play big in big games.'"

I loved it! Jay and I talked for hours, and the concept of parenting like a coach went from being an idea to a reality!

My next stop was the NFL Network. I secured an interview with NFL Network analyst Steve Mariucci, who is the former head coach of the San Francisco 49ers and the Detroit Lions. He is also the father of four. He explained:

> "Parenting and coaching are a lot alike because there are things common to both—you have to stay on both your players and your kids, you have to hold them accountable, and they both need to be respectful and always give their best effort with everything they do. All of those life lessons are the same."

A few days later, I received an email from the Baltimore Ravens. Head coach John Harbaugh granted me an interview! Next, I interviewed former Dallas Cowboys head coach Jimmy Johnson, Hall of Famers Troy Aikman and Howie Long, former Baltimore Ravens head coach Brian Billick, former head coach of the New York Giants Tom Coughlin, former head coach of the St. Louis Rams Dick Vermeil, former head coach of the Dallas Cowboys Barry Switzer, former Denver Broncos head coach Mike Shanahan (yes, they all have Super Bowl rings), and the list goes on.

From my research, I developed a parenting technique that I call *coach parenting*. Our preteens and teenagers face a myriad of pressures during adolescence—just when they are spending more time away from the nest. Your role as coach parent is to prepare your children to be independent and to make the right choices when you are not there to guide them. *The goal is not to control your children but to teach them how to control themselves.*

You can start coach parenting your teens at any time by adopting one, some, or all of the ideas you will read about. The younger your children are, the easier it will be. But if your sixteen-year-old seems out of your control, don't give up. Coach Johnson took the Cowboys from last place to the Super Bowl! It took two years of patience and hard work, but he did it—and he told me how you can, too! By implementing the techniques of coach parenting, you will parent with more confidence, command the respect of your home, and find more enjoyment in parenting your teenagers.

Coach Parenting teaches you how to help your teens become responsible, productive members of society (and of your family). Whether they are typical learners or face learning challenges, the system you will find in *Coach Parenting* will give your kids structure and stability so they can be the best they can be.

The season is about to begin. Grab your clipboard, make a game plan, and let's start coaching your team!

Chapter 1

THE KICKOFF—ASSUMING THE ROLE OF HEAD COACH

T he National Football League has thirty-two teams. Each team is made up of uniquely talented players and led by a head coach whose main responsibility is to help the team work together to make plays, score touchdowns, and win games. The head coach recognizes the strengths and weaknesses of the players and finds different ways to motivate them, knowing each player responds to a different approach. In addition to communicating effectively with players who are usually twenty, thirty, or even forty years their junior, a head coach must be able to effect change within the team, schedule every minute of the players' time, and ensure the players are studying and eating a proper diet. Wait—am I talking about an NFL head coach or me?

Football coaches are confronted with unexpected situations at every turn. They have to be master motivators, always watching, correcting, and pushing their players to be their best by using techniques they have mastered throughout their careers. Many of these brilliant coaches and their players have shared their secrets with me, so you and I can parent just like coaches coach!

The Coach Parent

The helicopter parent does their kids' homework, calls the teacher to get a grade changed, or tries to get the ballet teacher fired for not giving their child the lead in *The Nutcracker*. The *coach parent* uses the poor grade and the disappointment of not getting the part to impart life lessons on their teen. The free-range parent lets their teen come home when they want and set their own rules. The *coach parent* gives their teen structure by requiring them to adhere to a schedule, a curfew, and a code of conduct.

Jimmy Johnson, the former head coach of the Dallas Cowboys, explained,

> "I think the style that works best depends on your personality. Some people coach with fear and others are players' coaches, but no matter what your style, all coaches have to demand the respect of the players."

You do not have to change who you are or become a drill sergeant to be an effective parent. You have to implement a system where your kids follow your rules and respect the limits you set. They are older now (and possibly bigger than you are), so determining consequences for bad behavior is more of a challenge than just putting them in a time-out. Respect for your authority is the ultimate goal of the coach parent.

It's time to take over as head coach of your family! You will sweat the details, make a game plan for the season, and execute the plays. You can't cut, trade, or draft, so you have to work with the team you've got!

In the words of Super Bowl–winning head coach Dick Vermeil, "We gotta go to work!"

What Makes a Great Coach (or a Great Coach Parent)?

I asked broadcaster Bob Costas what he thought were the most important characteristics of a successful head football coach. He explained:

> "We associate the most successful coaches with three key elements: meticulous preparation, flexibility, and the respect of the locker room.
>
> - **Preparation.** You have to prepare because your opponent is prepared. You have to put in the pregame work and do the planning.
>
> - **Flexibility.** You have to have a willingness to adapt to your personnel. When Don Shula [former head coach of the Miami Dolphins] had a great defense and running game in Miami, he also had a Hall of Fame quarterback in Bob Griese. They threw the ball relatively infrequently, but given their overall strengths, they went to

three Super Bowls and had one perfect season. But after they got Dan Marino and a strong group of receivers, Shula was willing to adjust his approach to his personnel and the changing circumstances. Marino wound up throwing forty-eight touchdown passes in just his second season, and the Dolphins went to the Super Bowl again.

- **Respect.** A successful coach *has* to have the respect of the locker room. If not the love and affection of it, he has to have the respect."

Like a head football coach, you as the coach parent must also prepare your kids to the best of your ability, be flexible to the individual needs of each of your children, and command the respect of everyone in your household. This is no small task, especially if your teenagers have different interests and temperaments. To simplify this task, let's lay out your most important duties as head coach of your family.

Responsibilities of the Coach Parent

A head football coach creates a system where players can play to their strengths and improve upon their weaknesses. The system enables the players to take what they learn in practice and make the right decisions when they are playing a game. You, as the coach parent, will create a similar system with these elements:

- Clear-cut rules

- Defined expectations

- Pre-set consequences

This allows your teens to make their own choices within the boundaries of the system. As your children learn to exercise good judgment in precarious situations, the system gives them the strength to resist peer pressure and negative distractions in real-world situations that test or tempt them.

Remember, your teens are your rookie players and their greatest asset is their fearlessness. They are excited and ready to play but still lack the judgment and experience to call the plays.

Play to Win
When Bob Costas said successful coaches have "meticulous preparation," I sought the advice of Mike Shanahan, winner of two Super Bowls as the former head coach of the Denver Broncos—and highly regarded for his intense preparation. We talked about his experience coaching with his son, Kyle, who is now the head coach of the San Francisco 49ers.

> "When Kyle and I coached together, we would go through every situation. What would we have done differently if we had to do it over again? You try to eliminate mistakes. We would go through every situation on our side and the other side. We asked ourselves, 'Was this the best thing to do?' That's just preparation."

As a coach parent, you prepare your teenagers for situations they will face when you are not around. While you may think your kids would do the right thing when presented with a complex problem, many situations are not black and white.

Here are three scenarios your teenager may have or could encounter:

1. Your daughter's English teacher leaves the final exam in the lunchroom by accident, and your daughter sees the questions on the first page. Should she use that information to get a leg up or tell her teacher she saw it?

2. Your son's friend is the designated driver but has one beer at a party. Should your son still drive home with his friend?

3. A girl in your son's class sends him a topless photo. Does he share it with friends, keep it, or delete it?

You know the right choice in each scenario, but does your teen? That's where the preparation comes into play.

Coach Parent Preparation

Hot topics.

At the dinner table, discuss topics in the news. Whether it's a kid expelled for online bullying or an ethical dilemma facing the president of the United States, the newspaper is full of real-life situations people face every day. Debate them with your kids so they can think these through.

What would you do?
Give your kids hypothetical ethical dilemmas. Their responses may surprise you. If they come up with the less preferable choices, it's the perfect time to tell them why they should not cheat, why they should not get into the car with the friend who had a beer, and why sharing the topless photo is a bad idea.

Take a different perspective.
Coach Shanahan would review not only the plays of his own team, but also the decisions of the opponent in order to assume their perspective and understand why they made the decisions they did. Perspective-taking is an essential element in teaching your children how to treat others. While it could be amusing to poke fun at a friend's Instagram picture, your teen may not like it if it were done to them.

Adapt to Your Players

One of the toughest parts of coaching is working with the different personalities of everyone on your team. In your family, you may have three different children who need to be parented with three different approaches. Coach Mariucci noted the parallels between coaching and parenting.

> "Every athlete is different, just like every child is different. I have three boys and a daughter, and they each required different types of motivation and discipline. Some of my players needed a kick

in the butt, while others just needed some encouragement and a compliment."

To adapt your parenting style to each one of your kids, start with an even playing field and establish a few constants to work with both the sensitive child and the one who doesn't rattle easily.

Be Enthusiastic

As a full-time director of the Sports Academy at Brookwood Camps, former Miami Dolphins starting quarterback Jay Fiedler coaches tweens and teen boys and girls all summer long. During his ten-year career in the NFL, Jay played for many different coaches. He talked about his NFL experience and how he has brought that into coaching the kids in his camp.

> "When I played for the Miami Dolphins under head coach Dave Wannstedt, he was always enthusiastic. His message to us was that enthusiasm is contagious, even if it was false enthusiasm. Even if you were having a tough day and had to fake it, you had to fake that you were out there, ready to go in order to lift your teammates."

After speaking with Jay, I asked Coach Wannstedt why coaching enthusiasm was so important.

> "We accomplish more with a positive attitude. Enthusiasm is contagious, just like a bad attitude is contagious. As a coach, sometimes I had to force

it. If I wasn't excited, how could the players and other coaches be excited? And sometimes, in my heart, I *wasn't* excited, but it was my job to get my players enthusiastic and ready to work."

As a parent, it can be hard to be enthusiastic, especially when you have teenagers with the body clocks of a nocturnal animal. When your kids want to talk at 11:15 p.m., you may be exhausted, but you need to be there—excited to listen—when *they* want to share. It's during those times that you find out about their lives, their friends, and their hopes and dreams.

Show Your Love

If you watch the biggest, baddest head coaches and football players, they give each other hugs, pats on the back, and are not afraid to show affection.

Coach Vermeil, the former head coach of the Philadelphia Eagles, St. Louis Rams, and Kansas City Chiefs, was as tough a football coach as you could find. But he wasn't afraid to hug his players and tell them he loved them. This is his philosophy:

> "If they know you care, they will know you are doing it for all the right reasons. Very few people can give their best to those who care about them the least."

Often, we think to be firm we need to be distant or detached. But love and affection are key elements in coach parenting. If, by nature, you are not affectionate, let down your guard and say "I love you" when you hang up the phone or say good night. For dads: When you shake your son's hand, pull him toward you and give him a pat on the back. Put your arm around your daughter and tell her you are proud of her. For moms: Boys tend to shy away from mom's affection when they are teenagers, but you can tell them you love them and give them a pat on the back. If your daughter is not into being kissed by you, at least tell her how special she is to you. Showing love and affection gives your kids a valuable sense of security knowing you will always love them and be there for them.

Always Leave Them with Something

My neighbor is the mother of a lovable sixteen-year-old boy who is easily swayed by peer pressure. One night, he and his friends thought it would be funny to take some of the neighbors' trash cans and move them to a nearby pond. The cops caught them, and they were arrested. Any parent in the heat of the moment would want to lash out at those kids. But once they got arrested, it was pretty obvious to the boys that they had done a stupid thing.

Dr. Mark Unterberg, who was the team psychiatrist for the Dallas Cowboys from 1979 to 2009, described how a head coach would handle situations when a player made a mistake.

> "In my experience, the greatest coaches never took everything away from a player. They always left the players with something. If you get mad and tell someone they are a total idiot, the word *total* does not leave the person with anything. The good

coaches never did that. They knew if they did, the
player would feel humiliated and either fight the
coach or passively undermine the coach's effective-
ness to lead the team."

It's important to get angry with your children when they
do thoughtless things, so they know their actions are serious. You should also require them to face the consequences
for what they have done. But when the dust has settled, tell
them you know this was a mistake and not a reflection of
who they are as a person.

Pay Attention to Detail

The coach parent knows it's the little things that often matter most. Baltimore Ravens head coach John Harbaugh
emphasizes the importance of being disciplined when it
comes to small details:

"As a coach, discipline translates into everything
we do and how we coach our players. When we
are in practice, are we going to touch the line on
every drill? Because if you are half a step short in
the drill, then when it means the most, you will be
half a step short in the game."

If you see your teens acting more reclusive than usual,
dressing more provocatively, or spending time with friends
who may not be the best influence, take notice. Little
details now can become bigger issues later.

Simple steps such as looking at your daughter instead
of your email during halftime at her basketball game can

clue you in to a lot of pertinent information. Is she engaged with her teammates? Is she alone in her thoughts? Is she happy to be there, or does she seem to be left out of the team experience? The coach parent looks for insights into their teenager by observing at every opportunity and paying attention to small changes as they occur.

Tell Them Why

"Because I said so" may have worked for your parents' generation, but it doesn't work with Gen Z. Your kids were brought up with Google and are used to not just knowing "what" but also knowing "why" for everything! The head coach of the Minnesota Vikings, Mike Zimmer, shared the following:

> "I read a quote that leadership is getting them to *want* to do it, as opposed to telling them *to* do it. I try to find out what is important to the players and explain to them how they will be better by doing something. I get them to understand why, and I try to get them to see why it would help them. For example, I show the defensive line why they would do something so the linebackers have success."

Imagine your daughter wants to go to an unchaperoned party and gets upset when you say no. As a coach parent, you must explain that if the police bust the party and they find drugs or alcohol, the police can arrest everybody, even those not using drugs or drinking. An arrest could prevent her from graduating high school and getting into college. While your daughter will not be pleased with you for not allowing her to go to the party, the explanation gives her a reason to accept the limit.

Command and Demand

When head coach John Harbaugh started with the Baltimore Ravens, he had to unify a team that was not cohesive and give the players boundaries. My teenagers are always testing limits, and I asked him how he handles that issue with his players. He related a story about standing your ground without being confrontational.

> "At the Ravens, we had a dress code. Our record was 2–3 going to Miami, and guys were challenging me. One thing you can't do when you stand for something is you can't back down. You have to stand your ground. I had heard that Terrell Suggs and Antwan Barnes decided they would wear bright-white sneakers with their suits, which was not the dress code. You had to wear dress shoes. So, they show up about thirty seconds before the buses were about to leave, and I stood out there. They come walking up to me, and I'm not going to get mad because I know they are testing me. I can feel the buses almost leaning—everyone's noses pressed against the window as the team is looking on. I said, 'Hey man, you can't get on the bus with those sneakers.'
>
> Suggs said, 'I don't have shoes. So, what do you want me to do?'
>
> I said, 'Well, I guess you better have some dress shoes before the plane takes off, because you can't

get off the plane in Miami in those.' They rushed
home, got their dress shoes, and made it to th
plane. They get on the plane in dress shoes, an
everyone started clapping. It was a non-confro
tational confrontation. We dealt with the iss
and kept the personal stuff out of it. We confro
everything—not *everybody*."

As a parent, you have been in the position o
Harbaugh. Your teen knows the rules but tests y
if you will stand firm. Are you a coach parent w
business or will you crumble when they push ba

At the heart of these principles is a modern
of parenting. It's a hybrid of the old-school di
coach, the psychologically-minded coach who
to get into his players' heads, and the New
coach who cares about the mental and physica.
of his team.

Since every teen is different, you will determine which
methods your child needs more of and which ones are not
necessary. Do not try to change who you are or start parenting in a way that is inauthentic to you. Use every opportunity you can find to convey your values to your kids.

A head football coach does not create a winning team
in just a day. It takes countless hours of practice and
preparation. While every coach gets things done in their
own way, they all have the same end goal—making their
team into champions.

Chapter 2

...

CREATING A WINNING CULTURE

Football teams are known for their disciplined culture. Some teams have lots of rules that are strictly enforced, while other teams have a more player-centered culture with fewer rules and more focus on the needs of the individual player. There are coaches who are all work and no play and coaches who prioritize team bonding and having fun. Whatever the coaching style may be, it sets the tone for the team culture.

Creating a positive culture for the family can be challenging—especially when you have teenagers who think they have it all figured out. Here are a few things you will need to do to create a positive environment of love, stability, and safety where teenagers can thrive and be their best:

• Put the family first.

• Achieve the right balance of love and discipline.

• Take charge of the family schedule.

• Be consistent in your messaging.

• Hold everyone accountable for their actions.

Team First

Team first is one of the most important values of coach parenting. It means your home is a safe space for both parents and children. If you have a bad day at work, you don't yell and scream at your partner or your kids. *The peace and harmony of the family is more important than your bad day.*

When your teenagers get upset with you, they are not allowed to post something on social media to publicly humiliate the family. *The family comes before their momentary anger.*

There will be disagreements at home, but the culture of your family should come ahead of life's day-to-day conflicts. Getting your family to work as a team can be a challenge. I enlisted the help of Coach Mike Shanahan to understand how he kept his teams unified and working together.

> "Your job as coach is to let everybody know they have a role on the team. Everyone has to do their job. As coach, you talk to your players every day and convey the message—there is *nothing* more important than the team. If they don't have the discipline and can't adhere to the rules, the coach and owner need to let them know—because it's *always* team first if you want to win."

To relate Coach Shanahan's approach to family life, no one family member can be selfish and suck all of the air out of the room—including the parents. Here are three things you can do to put your team first:

- **Be private.** While you may have relationship issues with your spouse or partner, they should *not* be addressed in front of the kids.

- **Be unified.** Do not bad-mouth your partner or spouse to your kids. They should not feel they have to take sides.

- **Don't play favorites.** Allot special time with each of your children so every child feels they are an important member of the family.

Line Up Your Team

Like any great football coach, you have to evaluate what you have to work with and take notes! First, determine what kind of culture you have in your home at present. Do you all get along and laugh all the time? Is everyone shouting and slamming doors? Maybe a little of both?

As you observe your family, keep your eyes open for what you could be doing better as well as what triggers conflict in your family. If there is a lot of yelling, embarrassing one another, texting instead of talking, swearing, and distrust, the culture at home requires some work.

Work Together

Tom Coughlin, former head coach of the New York Giants and current EVP of football operations at the Jacksonville Jaguars, has walked into many situations where the team culture needed improvement.

"When you get a job with a football team, you are hired to correct a circumstance. You have to find people that will take your message into the classroom. When you go into a situation, you can't go in and be soft. You have to be hard and tough at first. You can always make things more forgiving going forward. It's not going to be easy. So, you must go in with structure."

To bring Coach Coughlin's experience into family life, everyone helping you raise your teenagers must be running the same play. For example, if your wife says your daughter cannot go to a party and you say, "Oh, don't listen to your mom, she is just being overprotective," your daughter learns she simply needs to go to you to get what she wants. This is detrimental to the family culture.

To change this pattern, parents and caregivers must stand together when a limit is set. If your teenagers are getting out of control, and they are defying you at every turn, tighten the reins and implement a swift consequence such as not giving them spending money or not letting them use the car. Once you see more respectful behavior and the home environment improves, you can ease up a bit.

Controlling the Play

If you are to implement a positive culture in your home, your kids have to listen to you and do what is asked of them. Former Dallas Cowboys quarterback Troy Aikman has experienced firsthand the importance of a head coach having control of his team.

"If a team doesn't respect the coach, it's anarchy. Regardless of how good of a season you are having, there is always a period where there is turmoil. You need a head coach who can command the room or you won't make it. There are young coaches who think their way to success is to befriend the players. They think as long as the players like them they will perform. That's not true. Players are motivated by different things."

Though your teenagers may be fun to spend time with, do not mistake them for your peers. Just because you can shoot hoops with them or see an R-rated movie together does not mean you are buddies. For the home environment to breed success, you must be an authority figure and implement three essentials:

1. Set goals.

2. Create structure by making a schedule.

3. Set expectations and consequences.

Set Goals

To implement a positive culture in your home, it's key to set goals as a family, so you are all working toward the same end. If you would like your daughter to be an actress, but she wants to go to medical school and be a pediatrician, you will never understand each other and will, likely, be at odds. If you want your family to eat dinner together every night without electronics, but your partner brings the cell phone to the table and emails through the meal, the environment will be hostile.

Coach John Harbaugh has an effective method he uses to help his team meet their common goals.

> "We have a saying at the Ravens. It's W.I.N.:
>
> **W**hat's
> **I**mportant
> **N**ow
>
> We have three goals each season—win the division, the conference, and the Super Bowl. But *what's important now* is how well we study our playbook, how hard we work in practice, and how much effort we put into everything we do. We have to take care of our business in the next hour. For example, if I am at the Masters, and I have to sink a three-foot putt to win the tournament, *what's important now* is that I hit a good putt and putt it straight. How I strike the ball is in my control, and it's *what's important now*. Where the ball goes is out of my control."

Like Coach Harbaugh, the coach parent sets a lofty goal for the family and then smaller goals to get them there. For example, if your son is getting a B in English, the big goal is an A for the year. *What's important now* is completing the homework properly, taking legible class notes, and studying for the quizzes and tests. Those are all in his control. What scores he gets on essays and tests are beyond his control. But if he focuses on *what's important now*, he has a better chance of achieving success.

Setting Family Goals

Goal cards

Have your teenager write down their short-term goals and their long-term goals on a card with today's date and the date they expect to meet their goal.

  Example:

  Long-term goal—Run a half marathon in thirteen weeks.

  Short-term goal—Run one mile in week one. Run two miles in week two.

  Each time a short-term goal is met, drop the card in a fishbowl. This is a visual reminder of the accomplishment, and it gives you a chance to tell them you are proud of them.

Incentives

Incentives will keep your teenager motivated. Make their favorite meal, treat them to a manicure, or let them sleep in instead of doing chores. Incentives acknowledge effort and progress. It's not about the prize but the recognition of the achievement.

Forward progress

Find an app that tracks the progress of the goal. For a fitness goal, a watch that counts steps can be a fun way to keep track of exercise goals.

What's Important Now

· · · · · ·

WIN

Daily Goals:

M	
T	
W	
TH	
F	

Goal of the Week:

Goal of the Month:

Game Week—Creating a Schedule

You've set your goals for the family. But how you get to those goals is where the team culture comes into play. The more predictability you can give your teens, the less anxiety they will encounter. You will also get less arguing and push-back from them because they will know what is expected of them.

Former New York Giants placekicker Lawrence Tynes found the structure of a set schedule always helped him as a player.

> "As pro athletes, we crave discipline. What I loved about playing for Coach Coughlin at the New York Giants was that every day was the same thing schedule-wise. I always knew everywhere I had to be and when. There was something calming about that. Athletes hate surprises."

Most people don't like surprises. While your kids need to be flexible, implementing a schedule helps them manage their time—not just for all the things they *have* to do, but for all the fun things they *want* to do as well.

The pro football week has a rhythm to it. On Monday, players and coaches review Sunday's game, watch film, lift weights, and work on correction. Tuesday is their day off, but they use it to get a jump start on their next opponents. Wednesday is the first official day of game week, where they make game plans and establish priorities. On Thursday, they work through the plan. On Friday, they practice their red-zone game plan. Saturday is walk-through and travel day if they have an away game. Sunday is game day. Players know what to expect and the kind of effort each day requires. *The schedule is not dictated by the players: It is made by the head coach.*

Your teenager's week should be equally predictable so they can learn to budget their time and set priorities. Your kids may give input, but the coach parent leads the team and sets the schedule.

The Family Schedule—How to Create It

1. Schedule the non-negotiables.

Enter these items first: school, exercise, homework, religious school, chores, play practice, sleep, etc.

2. Schedule mealtimes.

Your kids need to eat regularly and on a schedule so they are not skipping meals. Set mealtimes supply nutrition, stabilize moods, and provide your teens with energy.

3. Schedule time for fun.

Socializing, shopping, seeing a movie, going to a dance class, and playing a pickup game of basketball are downtimes for your teenager. Having fun helps them to relax and unwind.

4. Help your teenagers make a wish list.

What activities do your kids want to do but don't have the time for? Whether it's snowboarding, surfing, going camping, or painting, these activities take time and require planning.

Note: Take a look at your teen's phone usage. Eliminating time on Snapchat, Instagram, group chats, Netflix, and online games is a great way to find time for the wishlist activities.

Weekly Schedule

	M	T	W	TH	F	S	SU
7 AM	Wake up/shower/get dressed						
	Breakfast						
8 AM							
9 AM	School						Wake up/breakfast/shower/get dressed
10 AM							
11 AM						Wake up/shower/get dressed	Religious school
						Breakfast	
12 PM							Lunch with family
1 PM						Work out, play sports, hang out with friends	
2 PM							Homework, watch football, spend time with family
3 PM							
	Snack						
4 PM	Work out	Practice				Nap	
5 PM						Homework	
6 PM	Dinner with family					Dinner	Dinner with family
7 PM	Piano lesson	Homework			Hang out with friends	Hang out with friends	Homework, TV, relax
8 PM	Watch football						
9 PM	Homework	Read, watch TV					
10 PM							
11 PM	Get ready for bed						Bed
	Bed						
12 AM				Bed	Bed		
GOALS:	Get to bed by 11:30. Finish English paper.	Get to bed by 11:30. Finish physics lab.	Get to bed by 11:30. SAT prep.	Get to bed by 11:30. Study vocab.			

The schedule on the preceding page is for a sixteen-year-old boy. For a younger teen, bedtimes, homework times, and curfews will be different. Your child's schedule will also depend on the after-school activities they do, their age, and their interests. If they are younger, they may go to bed earlier. If they are older, they could have SAT prep. The key takeaway is the consistency in mealtimes, bedtimes, and family time.

Set Expectations and Consequences

Football coaches get the best out of their players by setting highly specific expectations for their players. Former Miami Dolphins and Chicago Bears head coach Dave Wannstedt felt he always had to be crystal clear with both his players and his children so they understood exactly what he expected of them.

> "In a team meeting, I would only give two or three points, so there was no gray area or misunderstanding. With your children, you have to be clear—'This is what we expect in school, when you are with your friends, and this is what you can and can't do.' No cloudiness. So they *can't* misunderstand you. If you are late, you are grounded just like if a player is late for practice—he doesn't play."

After I talked to Coach Wannstedt, my daughter and I were shopping with my girlfriend and her daughter. Both girls wanted Lokai bracelets. I told my daughter she already had five and could not have another one. My daughter was disappointed but let it go.

My friend told her daughter, "I don't know. Let me think about it. We'll see." My friend's response was not clear to her fourteen-year-old daughter. Was she going to get the bracelet or not? For the next half hour, her daughter worked on her tirelessly and, finally, my friend gave in. The message to her daughter was this: Mom will say yes if you bug her enough. There is no "We'll see" in football. Either you do the work or you don't play. Parenting should be equally clear.

Respect

One key element in creating a culture of respect is not allowing your kids to swear or talk back to you, your partner, or any other person in a position of authority such as a grandparent, teacher, or coach. Just one f*** you (even if they are hungry, tired, or upset) must be addressed. Pro football coaches do not allow players to be disrespectful to them or any other staff member, because it poisons the culture. I asked Coach Zimmer how he would handle a player speaking disrespectfully to one of his coaches.

> "I would interfere if a player yelled at a position coach. I'll discuss the situation and listen to both sides, but I would explain to the player why they can't be disrespectful to the coach and how it affects the team."

When your teenager swears at you or speaks to you disrespectfully, it affects everybody in the home and creates a culture of disrespect. If your teen has gotten in the habit of back talking and cursing at home, it's time to make some changes.

Steps for Dealing with Swearing

1. Talk about it.

When your teen is calm, explain that you are their parent, not a peer. Swearing at someone implies they are your equal, which you and your child are not.

2. Give a consequence.

During this chat, lay out the consequence should they swear at you again. After losing a few privileges like going out with their friends, playing sports, or having use of the car, the swearing will stop very quickly.

3. Follow through.

If they swear at you again, follow through on the consequence you laid out. Do not accept excuses like "I was hungry" or "You asked me to do that when I was in a bad mood." Swearing at you = consequence. No excuses.

4. Get some backup.

For moms: If your son is swearing at you, it can be helpful to enlist the help of a male figure your son respects, such as an uncle, a grandfather, or a sports coach. A man-to-man talk about why a real man does not swear at his mother can be just the help you need.

Show Up on Time or Get Benched

To create a culture of respect in your home, it's important that everyone's time is valued. Coach Coughlin insisted his players were not just on time but always five minutes *early*.

> "I want people who are hungry and anxious to get to work, to be the very best they can be so the organization can be the best it can be. You show me the quality of your enthusiasm and energy by being there early. When Michael Strahan showed up two minutes early for the team bus, he was really three minutes late by my watch. He often says that after his experience with me, he always keeps his watch *ten* minutes fast."

Steps for Punctuality in School

Arrival—If you take your kids to school, be sure they are on time every day. If they go on their own, wake them up earlier so they are not late.

Sundays—Go over the homework for the week with your teenager and help them determine what has to be done and when—so they can get everything done on time.

Consequence—If their assignments are handed in late, give a consequence at home.

Be Punctual—Lead by example and be on time for them as well.

Being on time gives teenagers a framework for their life and practice for their future. When kids are constantly late for school, late in handing in homework, or late for a curfew, it leads to poor organizational skills and misguided priorities. But, here's some good news. If you demand punctuality from your kids, penalize them for lateness, and encourage them to get things done ahead of time, you'll see a difference in behavior, a better ability to organize, and they will become more responsible young adults.

Curfew—Nothing Good Happens After Midnight

All teens need a curfew! A curfew sets an expectation and a limit that tells your child that although they may be bigger, stronger, or louder, they are accountable to you. It adds to the culture of respect in your home by showing them they need to adhere to the boundaries you have set.

What should that curfew be? Lawrence Tynes recounted what Coach Herm Edwards used to say to his players when he played for him in Kansas City.

> "When a player would get in trouble, Coach Edwards would come into a team meeting with a printout of the article about the player. He would put it on the overhead and read the article out loud, emphasizing to the guys that this happened after twelve a.m. and *nothing good happens after midnight.*"

I am a big believer that anything you can do after midnight, you can do before midnight. In light of that, here are some general curfew guidelines for teenagers. You can determine whether the times should be earlier or later depending on where you live and what kind of transportation is available to your child.

For Teenagers 16–18 in High School and Living at Home

If your teen is sixteen or older, they should be in by midnight. That may seem early to them, but you need your sleep, and so do they. If you live in a city with taxis, you may feel comfortable pushing it to 12:30. If they want to have friends over after midnight, that is a good option because at least you know your teen is safe in your home.

For Teenagers 13–15

Curfew should depend on the specific activity of the evening, but should not be later than 11 p.m. If teenagers are seeing an 8 p.m. movie that gets out at 10:00, and you are picking them up, then 10:00 p.m. is reasonable. If they are going to a party that celebrates a special occasion such as a bar or bat mitzvah, a quinceañera, or a sweet sixteen with adults, you can also make a judgment call based on when the party begins and ends. But if they're just hanging out with friends, curfew should be between 9:30 and 11:00 p.m., depending on your comfort level with where they are and with whom they're spending their time.

Consequence for Breaking Curfew

This curfew rule only works if there is a clear consequence for lateness. If your teen's curfew is 12:00 a.m. and they come home at 12:10 (even if there *was* traffic or whatever qualifies as an excuse where you live), then next week, curfew is at 11:40 p.m.—ten minutes earlier to make up for the ten minutes they were late, plus a five-minute penalty for every five minutes they were late. If curfew is broken a second time, they lose the privilege of going out the following weekend. To help heighten their awareness and increase their accountability, send them a text thirty minutes before curfew telling them they should start heading home.

No Excuses

There is always a reason why they didn't study for the test, why they didn't clean their room, why they left your car's gas gauge on empty, or why they missed the school bus. According to Jedd Fisch, offensive coordinator of the UCLA Bruins football team,

> "Excuses are reasons why someone fails."

When kids make excuses, they absolve themselves of responsibility and never learn where they went wrong. When you accept their excuses, they will continue to make up more of them. Coach parents expect their kids to take responsibility for their actions and correct their mistakes.

Always Demand Effort

Football coaches demand that their players give their best effort, and coach parents expect the same of their teenagers. That means laziness is never an excuse.

Howie Long, Pro Football Hall of Famer and lead analyst on the Fox Network, recalled a coach who shaped his work ethic.

"Michael Strahan and I both had defensive line coach Earl Leggett. We were both small-school guys, both second-round draft picks, and we both ended up having our measure of success. We were also both inducted into the Hall of Fame. Michael and I talk about Earl all the time. Earl had the ability to build a player from the ground up, taking his players mentally and physically to a place that you did not think you could go. In practice, each group did their own drills. We always laughed, and said if we survived the individual drills, practice was easy and the game was easy."

The job of the coach parent is to prepare your children to go into an unforgiving world so they are ready for anything. To make the game easy, the coach parent gives their kids the tools to behave like a professional in everything they do. If you ask them to clean their room, they clean it thoroughly, not just throw the laundry under the bed. If they buy you groceries, they come home and put them away neatly in the refrigerator instead of leaving them on the kitchen counter or in the trunk of your car to rot.

It's the coach parent's responsibility to require their children to complete tasks to the best of their ability. Of course, after a long day, the last thing you want to do is argue with your kids. But great coaches don't let up on their players because they are too tired to coach that day. They create a culture that values structure, discipline, consistent messaging, and great effort.

Chapter 3

...

THE BUY-IN

When a head coach starts coaching a football team, one of his first orders of business is getting the players to trust him and buy in to his style of coaching. He needs every player to believe his process will get them the championship they all seek. For you to be a successful coach parent, your family must *buy in* to your parenting approach. Everyone in your household has to trust you know what you are doing. But, how do you get their buy-in?

When Coach Jimmy Johnson first came to the Dallas Cowboys, the team was in bad shape. I asked his star quarterback, Troy Aikman, what Coach Johnson did to get the team to buy in to his system.

> "He cut players who did not buy in. Either you did your job or you weren't around. That put everyone on notice if you didn't do things the way he wanted."

Unlike in football, we can't cut our kids, so I posed this question to Coach Johnson: Would you coach a team differently if you could not cut your players?

"No, I would not. If they're mine, I'm gonna coach 'em the same."

Coach Johnson shows us that to be a great coach you have to be fully committed to each of your players and coach them no matter the difficulty. But he had a leg up on us parents. With a track record of success at the University of Miami, the Dallas Cowboys trusted he knew how to win. While you may not have the track record of Coach Johnson (unless you have an older set of great kids), your teens will buy in to your system if they trust your rules are for *their* benefit, not for *your* glory.

But we are parenting teenagers. They push back at every turn, sometimes just to be difficult. So, I sought Coach Coughlin's advice on how I could get the buy-in from my teenagers and get them to follow my lead.

"By knowing *you*. *You* have to be authentic. What must be taught has to be presented in the right manner. The basketball coach John Wooden said a pound of honey was much more valuable than a pound of criticism. You can motivate by being constructive, not just being critical. Everything you do is constructive criticism so players buy in and join."

Coach Coughlin shows us how a great coach gets the team to buy in by being true to their personal values and philosophy. If your children are not listening to you, you need to change your delivery—*not* your message. Along those lines, Coach Vermeil explains,

> "To be a great leader, you have to have a deeply ingrained leadership philosophy. A vision, values, and a process, along with a relationship-building program."

As the coach parent, you must know your core values and beliefs and then convey them to your kids so they understand how they will ultimately benefit by following your direction. That's where the buy-in comes into play.

Everyone's Running the Same Play

Imagine a football team where the offensive coordinator secretly tells the team to ignore the instructions of the head coach or the owner whispers plays to the quarterback. The head coach would have no authority, and the team would be in chaos.

If you, as the coach parent, set a rule, your partner, your mother, your brother, or whoever else helps you raise your kids may not contradict you in front of your teenager. They can tell you privately what they think but never in front of the kids. Everyone has to support the coach!

Mistakes Parents and Caregivers Make When Co-Parenting

- Telling kids they disagree with the parent who made the rule.

- Backing up the defiant teen with phrases such as "I would not want to do that either."

- Encouraging kids to keep secrets from their parents. Phrases like "Do not tell your mother I let you do this" or "Let's just keep this between us" tell the child it's okay to lie or hide things from the other parent.

- Bonding with the child by showing off past exploits. Telling the teen how you used to get high all the time (after the coach parent told them they were not to smoke pot) gives the child permission to ignore the wishes of the coach parent.

- Belittling the other parent in front of the child.

No One Crosses the Line of Scrimmage

In football, the line of scrimmage is an imaginary line across the field that neither the offense nor the defense can cross until the ball is snapped. It indicates to the players exactly where the play must begin. Coach parents give their teenagers lines they cannot cross and parameters for their actions. Giving teens freedom within clear-cut boundaries actually gives them a feeling of security and comfort even if they don't like or agree with the limits.

Setting Limits

Be specific. Teens have a short attention span. Be clear and to the point.

Do not manipulate. If you guilt them into doing something, you will become dependent on that tactic. They should do something because you asked them to, not because you tricked them into it.

Be fair. Give your teenagers the rules and the consequences ahead of time so they know the time if they commit the crime.

Follow through. If your teen breaks the rules, impose the consequence. This says, "I'm watching! You are important to me."

Setting Consequences

They can't earn it back. Home is not a prison: No one gets time off for good behavior. For every negative behavior, there is a consequence that is not up for discussion.

Be firm but not unreasonable. If you take away the phone, do it for a week, not a year. There has to be some light at the end of the tunnel.

Don't be cruel. Give consequences from a place of love. Do not shame, embarrass, or berate them. You are preparing them for life—not a lifetime on the psychiatrist's couch.

A placekicker knows the field goal structure is suspended ten feet above the ground, and the two vertical goalposts are eighteen feet six inches apart. He can practice kicking and get better each day because the goalpost is consistent. If he wants to work on kicking a fifty-yard field goal, the placekicker adjusts how far back he stands during practice and works on that skill. Now, imagine if the height and width of the goalposts were different on every football field. Without the consistency of the goalpost, the placekickers would not know if they were doing what they needed to do to be successful.

Kids, like athletes, need to feel limits from their parents. Boundaries provide your teenagers with a sense of security, show them you care, and give them a way to measure how they are doing. Providing your teens with straightforward dos and don'ts will ultimately get them to buy in to your system.

Don't Be Outcoached

Part of getting the buy-in is letting them know they can't outsmart you or wear you down. Teenagers are smart and know how to drive you crazy until you give in and they get their way. If they can "outcoach" the coach, you will never get the buy-in because they will not believe you will stand firm.

- **Avoid the talk trap.** When you set a limit, stick to it. No discussions. If you give in just once, your word is meaningless, and they will work on you even harder next time. If you don't budge, eventually they will get that "no" means "no."

- **Don't engage.** If your teen starts to argue with you, do not respond. If they want to go back and forth, they can join the debate team.

- **Channel your inner head coach.** If all else fails, think about what your favorite NFL coach would do if a player kept begging him to skip practice. Give in—or show him who's coach?

Get Open

To get your kids to buy in to your system, they need to know you are paying attention. Coach Mariucci felt it was important that both his players and his children knew he was always paying attention and available to them when they needed him most.

> "I came from a big Italian family. My mom would never go to bed until her chicks were in the nest. She would wait up for every one of us, ask about our night, feed us if we were hungry, give us a hug, and even put us to bed. Like my mom, I would always wait up until all four of my kids were home. I'd look them in the eyes, ask them about their night, and give them a hug. They knew I was there waiting. I wanted them to be accountable. It helped my kids make good decisions.
>
> In coaching, I did that too and tried to know what my players were doing. When I coached Brett Favre, I knew everything he did. (Well, almost!) I had spies follow him around town. They

would call me up and say, 'Hey Mooch, Brett is serving drinks at the local bar.'

I would say, 'Tell him to get home or I am coming down there right now.' Of course, I did not go down there, but I wanted him to know I had eyes everywhere."

From Coach Mariucci, we learn it's not enough to just stay up until the kids get home. Put on a bathrobe, say hello, give them a snack, and ask them about their night so there is no sneaking in. Yes, it's 12:15 a.m. and yes, you want to go to sleep, but they are wide-awake and want someone to talk to about their evening. Feed them, listen to what they did, and show them you care about what they care about. It will enhance your credibility with them and get the buy-in you need because they know you are there and eager to listen.

Be Aware of Your Blind Side

When it comes to our kids, it's easy to have a blind side and spin a situation in their favor even when they are wrong. For example, the teacher assigns an English paper that has to be exactly five paragraphs long. Your son writes six paragraphs and is penalized for not following instructions. It's easy to vilify the teacher for not appreciating your child's "creativity," but the truth is he did not follow the directions and deserved to be marked down. The blind-sided parent sees their son as the victim and emails the teacher. The coach parent points out that the directions were not followed and stands by the teacher.

Jim Harbaugh, the head coach of the University of Michigan Wolverines (and brother of John Harbaugh), has coached both NFL and college players. We discussed how he approaches both his children and his players.

> "It's good as a coach or parent to point out how what they have done was *the reason* they did not get the desired good result: You didn't listen, and you did not have the success you wanted. When you did it the right way, you did have success. Which would you rather have? Parenting and coaching is being there and knowing what's going on. You need to know what they did right and what they did wrong and then point it out to them."

When you take Coach Harbaugh's approach, you can overcome your blind side. Each scenario or interaction with your kids is an opportunity to point out how well they did, what they might have done differently, and how their actions led to the result.

Tips to Protect Your Blind Side

1. Be honest and objective.
If your teens did something right, compliment them on following instructions. If they ignored instructions, point out their responsibility in the poor result.

Continued

2. Don't jump to their defense.

When a teacher or a coach tells you something negative about your teenager, listen with an open mind so you can get to the bottom of it.

3. Avoid the "not my child" attitude.

Your kid may have been the one who put graffiti on the wall or instigated the fight. If you always take their side, even when they are wrong, they will continue to behave badly, believing you will bail them out.

Be Consistent

Every head football coach emphasizes the importance of being consistent when coaching their players. Whether it's coming to class prepared, working hard in practice, or simply showing up on time, giving players the same message all the time is what gives the team the structure they need to work to the best of their ability. Coach Wannstedt explained why this is such an important element in coaching.

> "My style was consistent. I always thought that one of the things we had to be (right or wrong) was consistent with how we treated situations. If there were consequences for being late, we had to be consistent with how we implemented that. We could not waiver for one thing or for one player."

For teenagers, being consistent in what you expect of them helps them achieve success. If you tell them they must do homework each night without their cell phone, and you do not waiver on this policy, they will know that checking their cell phone during homework time is not okay. If one night you say they can't have it, and the next night you change your mind and say they can have it, they will not know what is expected of them because you are not being consistent. This lack of structure makes you look unsure of yourself, which, in turn, diminishes their confidence in your leadership.

Nothing Personal

If you set up a system where every action has a clear consequence, when your teens break your rules, the punishment is for the action, not the person. Coach Coughlin explained,

> "You don't spend time criticizing the individual. You criticize a drill or an effort. You talk about what they do well, and then you criticize the effort in a way where they know you are very serious about wanting it corrected. You tell them you feel confident they can do better and you expect it to be better."

For example, you have made it clear to your teenage daughter that if she drinks, she won't be going out with friends for two straight weekends. One Saturday night, she comes home giggling, and you smell alcohol on her breath. When she is of sound mind, you don't criticize her or call her stupid for breaking the rule. Instead, you tell her she used poor judgment, drank after you told her it was unacceptable, and now she can't go out for two weekends. When she complains the punishment is not fair, you don't trust her, you treat her like a baby, and nothing she ever does is good enough for you, simply tell her you love *her*, but you do not love her drinking. She knew the consequence for breaking the drinking rule. It's not about her. It's about breaking the rules.

Walk the Walk

"Do what I say, not as I do" does not work for coaching or parenting. Your children will not buy in to your beliefs and values if *you* do not practice what you preach. Coach Mariucci explained how players often take their lead from their coaches.

> "To some extent, the players take on the personality of their coach. If a coach shows poise and humility when things are great, looks unflappable when things are unraveling, and he's remaining confident and doesn't doubt himself, players observe that and imitate that. If I would say to the guys after a win, 'We won a heck of a game and that was a *really* good team,' and give them a lot of credit, often the next day, I would read that quote from the players, so I knew they were listening. If we lost, I would say, 'Don't blame the official for that call; it's not about the one play.' Hopefully they will follow suit and think, *The coach said this, I should say this too.* If I were to storm off the field like a poor sport, my guys would think that's okay and might storm off the field too."

Coach Mariucci teaches us an important lesson in coaching and parenting. Your kids are watching you and they look to you to show them what is okay and what is not. If you want your children to listen to you, then you need to always be a role model to them and lead by example. If you mistreat a server in a restaurant, your kids will believe that it is appropriate behavior and do it too. If you show gratitude and thank the server for being helpful, your children will learn to show appreciation because of your positive example.

Believe in Them

Coach Zimmer recounted a personal story about his gridiron career and how the belief and faith from Hall of Fame head coach Bill Parcells changed how he perceived himself.

> "When I worked for Parcells, his office was next door to mine. I had never even thought about being a head coach. But Parcells would walk into my office all the time and say, 'Write this down! When you are head coach, remember this!' I would write all these 'Parcellsisms' down in a book that I keep in my office to this day. To have a Hall of Fame coach tell me those things and see the ability in me to be a head coach—when I didn't even recognize it in myself and didn't know what my future might be—made a huge difference in how I viewed myself."

You are your children's Hall of Famer—the person they look up to most. They will listen to you if they think you value their thoughts and their talents. Every time you encourage their efforts, you are telling them you are behind them and looking out for their best interests. When they feel you have faith in them, they will have faith in you. That is how you get them to truly listen to you and trust your judgment.

Without buy-in, your family can't work as a team. If you have been a lax parent before, it may take some time for them to understand things are going to change. Be yourself—just a little firmer or a little more understanding, depending on what your children need. Do not give up if things don't work right away. After they cross you a few times and see you will follow through on a consequence, they will get with the program, be more respectful, and do what is asked of them. While you can't cut your players, you *can* bench them and give them less independence. That is your leverage. They will still test you and try to sway you, but stay calm and consistent. It can take time before a team gets into a groove. But the buy-in is the first step toward success.

Chapter 4

...

THE GAME PLAN— COMMUNICATING WITH YOUR PLAYERS

Imagine you are an NFL coach with the most talented rookie quarterback in the league. The team owner will not allow you to trade this player even though he is moody, does not want to play your way, and thinks he knows better. The player constantly questions you and never takes no for an answer. As the head coach, your responsibility is to figure out how to get into your player's head, teach the plays, and get him out on the field to lead the team. The challenge here is communication. What do you have to say and how do you have to say it to get your point across?

Charlie Williams, the wide receivers coach for the University of South Florida, explained what he found to be the most effective method of communicating with his players.

"Be consistent with whatever you are teaching. Say the same things differently. For example, I might say to a player, 'Look the ball in, follow the ball all the way to your hand . . . ' I tell them the same things in different ways."

How you communicate with your teenagers is as important as *what* you communicate *to* them. Your four children may respond best to four different approaches. James Dunning, a parent coach for Pop Warner, AAU baseball, and AAA hockey for many years, shared his observations about coaching and communicating with kids.

"You can't homogenize the approach. You have to pick out what makes them tick. Just getting them to go on 3 instead of 2 and 1 can be a challenge. You have to look at how they learn and how they would grasp a concept or a football play. Some kids respond to it being drawn on a blackboard or notebook. Other kids would only learn if you walked through it and actually did it. Some kids would get it in concept if you explained it to them verbally, and they'd understand why they were doing it. Some kids had to watch other kids do it first and mimic it. As the coach, you have to relate to them on all these different levels of learning in a vocabulary that they understand."

The job of the coach parent is to figure out the best way to communicate with each one of your children. If one tactic does not work, you must try another, and another, until you figure out exactly what motivates them.

What's Your Coaching Style?

Every football coach, like every coach parent, has their own unique way of communicating. Sometimes the message is heard loud and clear, while other times, the players look at you as if you are speaking to them in a foreign language. To determine what kind of communicator *you* are, take this quiz and see what you find out.

Quiz—What Kind of Coach Are You?

1. **Your daughter did not study for her math test and received a C. You:**

   a. Look at her paper and berate her for being lazy.

   b. Ground her because she didn't study, but follow it up with a hug and tell her you know she will do better next time.

   c. Welcome her to the "C Club" and give her a high five for being average. After all, you never did well in math either.

   d. Look through the test, go over each mistake with her, and explain that mistakes are how you learn. Tell her not to worry about the grade because it's just *one* test.

2. **Your son is playing on his varsity basketball team. He gets his fourth foul and is thrown out of the game. He yells a profanity at the ref, takes off his jersey, and storms off the court. You:**

   a. Follow him out the door and yell at him for fouling out.

   b. Follow him out the door and insist he apologize to the ref after the game for his unsportsmanlike conduct.

   c. Yell at the ref for the bad call and leave the game with your son, all the while insisting the ref was an idiot.

Continued

    d. Follow him out the door and tell him you understand his frustration, but the ref takes time out of his own day to referee the game, and swearing at him is inappropriate. While you won't tell him what to do, you think he should go back in, apologize to the ref, and watch his teammates finish out the game.

3. **Your daughter speaks disrespectfully to her grandmother, who asked your daughter to take out the garbage while she was watching her favorite show. You:**

    a. Unplug the TV, get in her face, and go off on her for thirty minutes about why she can't talk to her grandmother that way.

    b. Tell her calmly that she may not speak to her grandmother that way, and, as a result, she won't be able to go out with her friends this weekend.

    c. Tell her you totally understand where she is coming from, and then instruct her grandmother not to bother her during her favorite show.

    d. Tell her she should pause the show, take out the garbage, and then go back to it. But first, she must apologize to her grandmother.

4. **Your son comes home at 1:00 a.m., ignoring his midnight curfew. You've been worrying for the last hour because he was not picking up his phone. You:**

    a. Stand in the driveway in your bathrobe waiting for him. When he gets home, he is going to be grounded for a month!

    b. Remind him that he must call if he's going to be late. Next weekend, he has to be back an hour earlier.

    c. You barely noticed. He is a boy. Let him have his fun.

    d. Give him a hug—thank God, he's home.

5. **Your son's screen time has been increasing, and he has been letting his homework slide. You:**

a. Shut off the Wi-Fi in the house, and tell him his work comes first.

b. Make him do his homework where you can see him to ensure he is not watching Netflix or playing video games.

c. Stay out of it. It's his problem.

d. School is hard! Sit with him and help him with every problem.

Results: Give yourself the following points for each of the answers you chose:

a. 5

b. 4

c. 0

d. 3

0–10 points—You are a Buddy. You are your teen's friend. You get where he/she is coming from and value your friendship with him/her over your role as disciplinarian. You always take your kids' side and think they do no wrong. Your child may have high self-esteem, but don't be surprised if you end up with a self-centered, undisciplined teenager who feels entitled to talk back to family members, teachers, and coaches.

10–20 points—You are Competitive. You're responsive *and* authoritative. Your discipline methods are supportive rather than punitive. You listen, but have expectations for good behavior. Your kids tend to be responsible and think for themselves.

20–25 points—You are Authoritarian. You are a strict disciplinarian coach. You are highly directive and have clear rules for your child's behavior. Punishment is swift, discussion rare. Your kids sometimes obey out of fear but not always out of understanding.

The Importance of the Individual

While most football coaches have the same rules for everyone on the team, they coach different personalities in different ways. To get the most out of their players, they find the communication style that resonates with the individual they are coaching. Coach Zimmer explained how he works with the varied personalities on his team.

> "I had one player who never wanted to be embarrassed in front of anybody else. So, I would always walk over, put my arm around him, and say, 'This is how I want you to do this.' And then you have players that you have to continually push, and I am hard on them. Some take it better than others. You have to try to figure out what buttons to push."

Coach Zimmer's approach works well for a family because no two children are alike. The following techniques will give you an array of options to communicate effectively to both your toughest and your most sensitive child. Try the ones that feel most natural to your parenting style and personality. Make note of what each of your children responds to best and incorporate it into your parenting going forward.

Go Where Your Player Needs You to Be

Because every child has different emotional needs, you have to adapt to the individual needs of each of your children. Coach Johnson related how he handled the teams he coached.

> "I told every team, 'I am going to be very consistent. I am going to treat every one of you differently.' How

I treated them was based on how hard they worked, how they met the rules, how they did what I asked them to do, and how good a player they were. So, if a player wasn't so good, and didn't do what I asked, I cut him. But if they were great players, if they happened to slip up on occasion, I'd let it slide."

Howie Long, who has worked with Coach Johnson for Fox Sports for many years, explained it like this:

"Jimmy Johnson says you can't coach everyone the same way. I think my son Kyle [guard for the Chicago Bears] reacts more to what you say, so you have to be more mindful of how you approach him. Chris [defensive end for the Philadelphia Eagles] is like a shark. The line is very flat. No ups and downs. Anyone who has multiple kids knows all of them are different."

In your home, you may have one child who is always respectful and does what they are told and another who comes home late without calling. If one night your "respectful" child forgets to call when they are late, you are not going to be as hard on them as the child who is constantly acting irresponsibly and ignoring your rules. It would be unfair to treat them exactly the same.

Be Funny
Humor can be an effective way to convey a serious message. For example, Coach John Harbaugh has a terrific sense of humor, and he shared how he incorporates it in his coaching.

"You have to use humor because you have to have fun. When you stand in front of that team, you have to be intentional. You have to convey the idea of playing smart, not doing dumb things, or getting foolish penalties for punching somebody. So, we started showing videos of people doing stupid things that were funny—like skateboarding down a flight of stairs or something silly like that. Terrell Suggs calls it 'Don't be an idiot.' We show this video at the end of a team meeting to convey the message of 'Don't do something stupid.' But instead of lecturing everybody, it's a three- or four-minute laugh session and everybody loves it."

I love using humor whenever I can. There was one time when my husband and two kids kept leaving their shoes under the dining table during dinner. One night, I wanted to have a little fun with them, so I set three extra place settings with plates full of food at the table. But their plates were empty, and their shoes were under the table where they left them the night before. My daughter asked who would be joining us for dinner. I said, "Oh, they are already here."

My son said, "What do you mean? There is no one here."

To which I replied, "Don't you see the invisible man and his invisible kids? Their shoes are under the table." We had a good laugh about it, and they got the message not to leave their shoes under the table anymore. It was also more fun for me than nagging them to put their shoes away.

Don't Make Empty Threats

Coach parenting is all about the follow-through. Don't say it if you aren't prepared to do it. When you get mad, it's tempting to threaten to kick them out on the street, to throw their computer out the window, or to smash their phone. Barry Switzer, the former head coach of the University of Oklahoma Sooners and the Dallas Cowboys, explained,

> "As long as the players believe in you and know you have an interest and you give them tough love, you can be demanding of players. You can show them you love them. But you *have* to follow through. You *have* to do what you say you're gonna do!"

That's why it's never a good idea to threaten to break expensive items such as electronics because it's a threat you won't want to carry out. Your kids will need those things later, and it will cost you money to replace them. Your teen also knows you probably won't do it, so they don't take the threat seriously.

Threatening to throw your child out of the house is another poor parenting tactic. Are you really going to kick them out and then worry what happened to them the entire night? It's an empty threat, and they know it. (If the behavior is so bad you need to throw them out, then more extreme measures must be considered, such as professional help or a residential program that can help them work through their issues.) Whatever you say you are going to take away, be prepared to do it when they defy your wishes.

Tell Them the Truth

Pumping up your children with false compliments is not preparing them for life. When they realize you were lying to them, they will distrust you and even resent you for setting them up for failure. Placekicker Lawrence Tynes talked about how he appreciated the honesty of his New York Giants head coach, Tom Coughlin.

> "He was black and white. My first year, I struggled. He called me to his office and said, 'You have to do better or you are not going to be here.' He lets you know where you stand. I can respect that."

If you know telling the truth will make your child feel bad, start with a positive. For example, your son loves to sing and wants to try out for *The Voice* but doesn't quite have the chops for it. You could say, "You are such a great performer. I know you love to sing, and you should keep practicing. Instead of trying out for *The Voice*, why not work to expand your vocal range and try out for a local competition first to see how it goes?" You are encouraging him without giving him false hope.

Be Willing to Change Your Formation

My son played a varsity basketball game and they suffered a big loss to their rival school. As soon as we got in the car, I started discussing the game with him, going play by play. He hadn't cooled down from the emotions of the loss and did not want to hear any of it, especially from me. Clearly, I brought it up way too soon, and he got upset with me. I knew I made a mistake but was not sure what to say to him. I asked the head coach of the Dartmouth College Big Green football team, Buddy Teevens, how he tells his team when he's made a mistake.

> "I say, 'I blew that call.' When you show you are human and are not afraid, they appreciate that. I make a mistake, resolve it, and talk it through."

After talking to Coach Teevens, I apologized to my son for being insensitive and told him how sorry I was for not giving him his space after the game. He was appreciative of my apology and, in turn, said he was sorry for snapping at me. Then we discussed what the loss meant to him, his frustration with his performance, and how he could have done some things differently. From this experience, I learned where I went wrong and how to better handle this situation in the future.

Be Positive

Unfortunately, kids remember negative comments more acutely than positive ones. If you have to make a negative comment, it should be to help make a change—not to get them upset and have them lose confidence. Coach John Harbaugh shared a lesson he learned from the owner of the Baltimore Ravens.

> "The owner of our team, Steve Bisciotti, has a 9 to 1 principle. In football, we correct, we fix, and we need to improve weakness. We always hit people with the thing they need to do better. So, it ends up that 90 percent of the time players hear what

they are *not* doing well, and they think all they ever hear is the bad stuff.

You want to put the correction in context. You have to say, 'I get you are doing 90 percent of things right. You just need to work on 10 percent of things to do better.' They say, 'Yeah, I can see that.'

But it takes a lot more work on the part of the coach. You have to do 90 percent more work because you have to point out the 90 percent they are doing *right*—not just harp on what they are doing wrong."

After my talk with Coach Harbaugh, my daughter got upset with her friend on Instagram. I wanted her to remove a comment she made, so I decided to try Coach Harbaugh's approach to the issue.

Instead of just telling her I did not like her comment, I explained that although she made a mistake in *this* instance, she usually shows so much kindness to her friends, especially when they need her help. I then listed nine kind gestures she had done for her friends over the past few months.

After we talked, she removed the comment. She said, "Mom, didn't I handle it well?" When I saw her look to me for approval, I knew an extra bit of praise would instill the lesson I sought to teach.

I said, "Yes, it is always difficult to admit to a mistake, but once you do, and you fix it, everyone feels so much better. You should be really proud of the young woman you have become." We have not had an Instagram issue since then, so it looks like the 9 to 1 principle took!

Use Affect

In psychology, the word *affect* refers to emotion and feeling. We use affect to differentiate how we feel by varying our tone of voice and our physical gestures. For example, when a mom screams at her son for pulling his sister's hair, the tone of voice she uses communicates to her son that he's doing something wrong. If she later uses that same tone of voice when he spills a glass of juice by accident, she is not using affect consistently or appropriately.

When you see football coaches on the sidelines at a game screaming and yelling, it seems like a good coach needs to yell a lot. However, what we are seeing doesn't reflect how they coach on a day-to-day basis. They are reacting to the emotions of the game. I asked Dr. Mark Unterberg whether it's okay to yell and scream sometimes or show anger when you are a parent. He said,

> "The successful coaches know how to use affect (anger), but not in a manipulative or excessive way. If someone was doing something wrong, they would reprimand the player with sternness, but would follow it with praise. Some parents are afraid to get furious. But affect—the feeling state—can be an important component in getting across a message."

Depending on the personalities of your children, use your tone of voice to let them know when they are doing well and when they need to do better. For a more sensitive teenager, a simple change in your tone lets them know you are not pleased. For a child who doesn't take things all that seriously, you may need to get in their face a bit and express anger through gesture and raising your voice. The end goal is for your children to understand the difference between when an action is serious and when it is excusable.

Get Emotional

Coach Vermeil believes it is good to be emotional if that is how you are, and to let your team know how you feel.

> "I read this slogan and adopted it: 'There is a big difference between being human and being a human being.' When you're a human being with them, they see you as you really are, whether you are emotional or you are livid. It doesn't mean you don't love 'em when you're upset with them, but if you are upset, they need to know it."

While screaming and yelling may not be your personal style when you are really upset, it can be an effective communication tool. When your child has done something really wrong, you cannot hold back because you fear upsetting them or even making them cry. Sometimes, they *need* to cry and feel remorse. Feeling ashamed can teach them a valuable lesson and prevent future bad behavior. My mother always told me, "It's better you cry than I cry, because when a parent cries, something has gone terribly wrong."

Find an Opening

The key to great communication with your teen is connecting with them on what interests them most. When former New York Giants running back Tiki Barber was working on his technique to avoid fumbling, one of his coaches approached him in a unique way.

> "Jerald Ingram, who served as the running backs coach for the New York Giants, knew me well. He knew if he challenged me on something like fumbling from the point of view of physics or the actual mechanics of carrying a football rather than like a phys ed major, I would be interested. When he explained it to me in terms of mass and acceleration, it caught my attention right away, and I was obsessed with studying it. So, what I did to fix the fumbling was mechanical, and it worked for me because I enjoyed studying how to fix it. Coach Ingram was able to channel the math/science guy in me to make me a better football player."

I love Tiki's story because it illustrates how a great coach figures out what makes their player tick—what excites them and makes them want to learn. With my son, basketball has always been his thing. When he had to come up with a science fair experiment, he got excited about calculating the mean of how high the players on a given team could jump. Even when we discuss drugs and alcohol, I always bring it back to his desire to play college basketball because drug use and excessive consumption of alcohol will destroy his body and his competitive edge. I use *his* dream of playing basketball as his incentive to resist peer pressure. No matter what the scenario, I know if I somehow relate it to basketball, he gets it.

Your teen's interest is always your way in. If you know or can work to figure out what gets them excited, you can use it to convey any message you want.

Create a "Locker Room"

Every family needs a "locker room." It's a no-man's-land in your home where everyone is welcome. Your kids' rooms and your bedroom should be personal space. The kitchen or family room is the perfect place to create a casual atmosphere where face-to-face communication happens. If you have a space like this in your home that has potential, transform it into your locker room. It will be the place where you learn, listen, observe, and get all the information you need to help your teens grow and flourish.

Coach Wannstedt said he felt it was important to always create a space for his team where everyone could come together and bond, especially when they were on the road.

> "I used to try to create situations when we would travel where we would have team meals together. I always tried to put our players in an environment that cultivated conditions for them to be together. I tried to create an atmosphere where they could bond. As a parent, as well as a coach, you have to create situations where you can initiate communication."

The idea behind the "locker room" is to have a place where the family can communicate and spend time together. Parents and children need to interact with one another on a daily basis and not from behind a screen. The locker room is all about the exchange of ideas and the connection.

My kitchen is our locker room. I have a table and chairs where we can share a meal or snack and do homework when necessary. For your team, here are some ideas to create your own locker room, both inside and outside your home.

Feed the Team

The easiest way to get your teens talking is to feed them. My kids love my homemade chicken soup with noodles and my lasagna. I make eight containers of chicken soup at a time and freeze it so it's always available. I also have a foolproof lasagna that I can make quickly or keep in the freezer. It satisfies the hungriest teenagers, and when they smell it being prepared and cooking in the oven, they hover nearby until it's ready.

Erika's Game Day Lasagna

1 (16-ounce) package lasagna noodles
1 (26-ounce) jar pasta sauce
4 cups shredded mozzarella cheese
½ pound fresh baby spinach
½ cup grated Parmesan cheese

Cook the lasagna noodles in a large pot of boiling water for 5 minutes so they are not too soft. Rinse with cold water and drain.

Preheat oven to 350°F (175°C). Spread 1 cup of the pasta sauce on the bottom of a greased 9x13-inch baking dish. Layer the lasagna noodles, sauce, shredded mozzarella cheese, and spinach. Repeat the layering and top with the remaining mozzarella cheese and the grated Parmesan cheese.

Bake, uncovered, for 40 minutes. Let stand 15 minutes before serving.

Tip: If you don't have much time to cook, your local pizzeria can make you large platters of chicken parmigiana, baked ziti, and meatballs to keep in your freezer.

Host the Players

Be the home where kids are welcome and where they all want to go. When your children's friends want to be at your house, it's a great way to get to know them and observe them. When your kitchen table is the "locker room," you can be in the background making food, folding laundry, or paying bills. I love talking to my kids' friends and asking them questions about school, what they are doing over the summer, or any other topic they might bring up. Just the other day, my son told me I was considered "everyone's mom" because all his friends know me and feel comfortable confiding in me. My motto: *"If you feed them, they will talk!"*

Put In a Charging Station

Everyone likes to have a fully charged phone, tablet, and laptop. Take advantage of that by having a designated charging area in your "locker room" with multiple chargers available for anyone who wants to use them. Remember, if the phone is charging in the corner, it is not in your kid's hand, which means they have to look up and have an actual conversation with you without the distraction of the texts and Snapchat stories every other minute.

Keep the Locker Room Open After Hours

Since my kids are teenagers, they are up late doing homework. Before they go to bed, we sit in the kitchen and have a cup of tea (or in the case of my teenage son, a second dinner) and we catch up on the day without the distractions of the phone and emails. Sometimes, it's the only quiet time we get to talk.

Locker Rooms Can Be Portable

The car is another great locker room. Sometimes, it's best to say no to the carpool just to have that twenty minutes of alone time where your kids can talk about whatever is on their minds. It also gives them some quiet time before and after an activity.

My teenagers like to sit in the front seat so they can be the car DJ and show me what new songs they like. Having them next to me makes it easier to engage in conversation. If they are in the back, it's hard to hear them, and they are only half paying attention because the phone is occupying them.

Note: To make the locker-room concept truly successful, it has to be a no-judgment zone. Everyone should be able to speak freely. Anything you or your teenagers say should be kept confidential and never be brought up at a later date to embarrass or make fun of anyone.

The Team Meal

Coach Wannstedt felt that eating meals together was a wonderful way for players to bond when they were not working. When I was growing up, we always ate dinner together, and I believe it is one of the most important goals for families. With all the distractions in our lives, it's easy to neglect this fundamental part of family time. There are even studies linking family mealtime to a host of positive outcomes, as this excerpt from an article by Anne Fishel in *The Washington Post* indicates:

Studies link regular family dinners with lowering a host of high-risk teenage behaviors parents fear: smoking, binge drinking, marijuana use, violence, school problems, eating disorders and sexual activity. In one study of more than 5,000 Minnesota teens, researchers concluded that regular family dinners were associated with lower rates of depression and suicidal thoughts. In a very recent study, kids who had been victims of cyberbullying bounced back more readily if they had regular family dinners.

Good communication starts with taking a time-out from your busy life and sitting down to a family meal. While family mealtime can be difficult due to conflicting work schedules and extracurricular activities for the kids, if you can start with just one meal a week together, you will see an improvement in your family life and communication.

To maximize the benefit of family mealtime, try implementing these rules.

1. No electronics at the table.
This means no cell phones, iPads, or laptops are permitted. Dinner should be about conversation and eating—not Twitter or Instagram feeds. The TV should not be on either, because it if is, no one will be talking.

2. Good table manners are expected.
Add a bit of formality and respect to your table. Everyone must use a fork and a knife, have a napkin in their lap, and keep their elbows off the table.

3. Everyone will be properly dressed for dinner.

It's okay to be casual and comfy, but that doesn't mean teens can get away with being gross. Coming to the table in boxers and shirtless is a no-no.

4. Dinner means a nice meal.

It's tough enough to get the family to eat dinner together. If it's not presented nicely or doesn't taste great, it makes it even harder. Figure out what the family likes and how to get it on the table. If you are a lousy cook or don't have time, plan your meals ahead to make them memorable for your kids. Your teens will remember the table you set and the meals you serve when it comes time for them to start entertaining on their own. The care you put into their meals won't be forgotten when they have guests they want to impress.

How you communicate, where you communicate, and when you communicate with your teenagers is as important as *what* you communicate to them. While some kids respond well to a kind, gentle tone, others need more of a verbal kick in the pants. If your teenager is not getting your message, find a better way to say it. If you are not connecting with them, share a meal and ask them about what interests them.

It is not their job to get your message. It is your job to figure out how to get them to get your message. Whether it's at the dinner table, having a midnight snack, or during the car ride to school, try to connect with them every day and get them talking. With these tools, you can coach them to play the game of life to their best of their ability.

Chapter 5

...

HALFTIME ADJUSTMENTS

By now, you have put your game plan in place. You have set expectations and consequences, created structure in your home, and worked on how to better communicate with your kids. You should be feeling pretty good. Your tenth-grade daughter is getting good grades, has a nice group of friends, and is on the dance team.

But like in a football game, momentum can swing wildly from the first quarter to the second quarter—and with just fifteen seconds left on the clock, your ball is intercepted: Your daughter has fallen under the spell of her senior boyfriend who is too cool for school, texts her all night, and wants her to wear those bandage dresses with ankle boots.

It's halftime, and you need to rethink your game plan if you want to keep your daughter from giving back all the gains she has made. But how do you combat an opponent who won't let up and seems to have the upper hand?

This is where the halftime adjustments need to be made. Remember what Bob Costas said about great coaches being flexible and adjusting to the environment, the times, and the personnel? You're the coach parent now, and you have to think on your feet when your adolescents are tempted by influences that can lead them down paths you never anticipated. You need to figure out how to motivate them in different ways, because they are getting older, and the stakes are getting higher.

Even the toughest football players do not like to be criticized or corrected. The way you confront them can inspire them to make a change or shut them down completely. I discussed with Coach John Harbaugh how he addresses his players when he wants them to change course.

> "When you confront them, they will get emotional and push back. But, it's about trust, and trust is based on honesty. You can lose it quickly if your motives are dishonest. When the players get hurt and are sensitive, they will lash out. If you stay consistent and frame it as *this is where we are going, and this is how we get there*, they will understand you better."

How to Critique Your Players

Coach Harbaugh's approach centers around the concepts of motive and honesty in confronting a player. When you think of the example of the teenage daughter and the boyfriend you don't like, you need to ask yourself three questions before addressing the situation:

1. What is my motive?

2. What is my end goal?

3. How do I make the situation better, not worse?

To motivate your teens to make changes in their behavior, work ethic, and attitude, first look inside yourself and understand your intentions. Do you want your teens to change because it will help *them*, or is it more about their actions reflecting badly on *you*? If you are concerned your children's behaviors are a poor reflection on you, then your motives are self-serving, and your kids will see right through that. They will rebel and go even further away from where you want them to be.

In the case of your teenage daughter, if you approach her and tell her how embarrassing it is for you that she is dating this guy and that she is never allowed to see him again, the forbidden fruit will be so much sweeter. She will lie, sneak out of the house, and find ways you cannot even conceive of just to be with him. He is giving her a type of attention you cannot, and nothing blinds a teenage girl like being in love.

So what do you do when you need to change course? First, go back to the end goals you agreed upon with your kids, show them how you want to help them get there, and then discuss with them the path to success. Then, try some coach parenting techniques to help you combat peer pressure, thrill seeking, and even the negative effects of young love.

See Their Point of View

Kids are smart, and they know when they are being manipulated. Dr. Unterberg talked about how important it is to respect where a person is before being critical of them.

"The most effective coaches believe in the intelligence of the players and respect the intelligence of the players. The coaches that had difficulty were the ones who 'dummied down' on players. When they had that attitude, it would hurt the feelings of the players. When you talk about teenagers, though they are not adults, they are on their way. I think you respect where they are in their lives and respond based on their unique struggles."

Let's return to the example of the teenage daughter who has fallen for the senior. Before confronting the situation, it's important to understand how the attention of this boy is making her feel. While you see a host of negatives like distraction from schoolwork, sexual experimentation, and relationship drama, she is feeling desired, and she's excited about being in love for the first time.

Rather than being critical, first validate her feelings and make her feel that you understand her. Tell her about the first time you fell in love and what you experienced both positively and negatively. As you discuss the situation with her, see if she can point out what could happen if she spends too much time on the phone and doesn't get her homework done. Discuss the sexual situations she may find herself in, and talk to her about what she is comfortable doing with this boy as well as his possible expectations of her.

If you can see the situation through her eyes and relate to her on that level, she is more likely to listen to you when you express your concerns. While it could be tough to get her to break up with the boy, at least you can get her to think before engaging in situations she is not ready to handle. As you speak to her, asking questions is always better than lecturing. Ask her how she will feel if he takes her to a party where she is the only sophomore, if he drives too fast with her in the car, if he wants to get more intimate than she does, et cetera. If she can recognize the potential dangers from her own point of view, you will make more headway with her, and she will be less likely to hide things or lie to you.

Be Everybody's Coach

Most kids (and most adults) don't like being directly confronted about something they have done or may do. But it's human nature to enjoy talking about what *other* people are doing or may do. So, why not capitalize on that? A message is often better received when it's given to everyone in a group instead of singling out one person. If your teenager can learn something without having to make the mistake themselves, think how valuable this could be.

Brian Billick, former head coach of the Baltimore Ravens and current NFL Network analyst, liked to use other teams as examples of what not to do.

> "When you get an example from another team and you can teach a lesson from their mistake, that's a great way to teach. Like when some player was being selfish, I would show it to my team and say, 'What is this guy trying to accomplish and is he doing it?' A classic example was when [the Pittsburgh Steelers' wide receiver] Antonio Brown taped [head] Coach Tomlin's locker room speech and live-streamed it. In a case like that, I would go

to my team and say, 'Tell me that you recognize this was a mistake.' If they don't see it, then we have to address that."

Coach Billick's idea is an effective way of conveying a lesson to your kids without them feeling you are preaching directly to them. He is using someone his players know, respect, and identify with to teach his players what not to do. Nobody feels singled out and everyone can rally around why what this player did was wrong. It makes them feel good about not using poor judgment, and it also sends a message that live-streaming a private speech is not acceptable to the team.

To bring it back to teenagers, my friend's thirteen-year-old daughter got into a car with a sixteen-year-old boy from school who had just gotten his license, and they got into a minor fender bender. Rather than lecturing my daughter about the dangers of getting into a car with a young driver, I waited until she had some friends over.

I told them all the story emphasizing the danger of driving with a boy who was so inexperienced. Remember—to a thirteen-year-old girl, a sixteen-year-old boy is someone to look up to, so it wasn't surprising when they didn't see anything wrong with driving with a boy who just got his license. This was the perfect opportunity to explain to them how having a license does not necessarily make you a good driver. When I drove the girls home, I pointed out how other drivers cut you off, don't signal, and pull out without looking. The girls got the message, and no one felt singled out or lectured.

Give the Right Incentive

When kids are little, we give them a lollipop or a new toy to incentivize them or reward them for good behavior. But as they get older, kids will want more. So if you promise them a new phone if they get an A, next time they'll expect a new computer, and then a new car, and soon, the sky is the limit. Sometimes, giving them a simple compliment, which is something every teenager craves and every parent can afford, is just what they need.

Kenneth Tinsley is a college wide receivers coach. Before football, he coached my son in basketball, and I was impressed with how positive he was with his players. They all wanted to work as hard as they could for him.

> "I get so excited when my players do something right. I always congratulate them, especially on the little things. If you do that, they will want to do it over and over again."

With this in mind, when your child writes a great essay, does their chores well, or is even nice to their sister, give them a compliment. It is often a better incentive than anything money can buy.

Ask Questions

Your son gets in a fist fight in school. You're upset because he let someone provoke him when he could have just as easily walked away. It's easy to admonish him for the fight, but that doesn't address the problem of him fighting. When I asked Coach Billick how we can get our teenagers to correct their mistakes, he suggested,

> "Ask them, 'How could you have done that bet-
> ter? How should you handle that next time?'
> When you approach it that way, you give them
> the respect they deserve. You may have a specific
> idea. You know why they're struggling—but you
> let *them* get to it. You help steer them toward the
> right answer. They give you a few answers, and
> you say, 'I think you may want to focus on that
> last one.' If you let them come around to it, you
> can get them to say what you want them to say."

In the case of your son who was fighting, ask him how he felt after the fight, if he thought it accomplished anything, and if there was a way he could have avoided it. When he comes up with the answers on his own, he is more likely to realize where he went wrong and find a better solution the next time he is provoked.

Be Demanding

When teenagers are in a slump academically, emotionally, or physically, getting them to change their ways is never an easy task. How does the coach parent get extra effort out of their child? Coach Johnson believed he had to set the bar high for his players to get the most out of them.

> "I always felt like if the player respected me, and I
> had credibility, I could demand a lot. You get them
> in a habit of giving extra effort."

Parents have built-in credibility with their kids just by being their mother and father. You can capitalize on that and teach them to make a habit of working their hardest. If you are going to demand a lot from them, they need to feel you are paying attention when they give it their all. That means reviewing their work, noticing when they do things well, and correcting them when they go off course. If you get lax and stop paying attention, don't be surprised if they don't step up.

Avoid the Fumble

The team is down at halftime due to several interceptions the quarterback has thrown. Imagine if the head coach had been scrolling through Facebook, texting photos of fans with painted faces to his friends, or taking selfies all through the second quarter. How could he know what adjustments to make? Parenting, like coaching, requires laser focus and attention to detail.

Quarterback Jay Fiedler tells a story about when he played with the Minnesota Vikings for coach Denny Green.

> "We were getting toward the late half of the season in Minnesota. The night before Sunday's game, he told us how he was going to the airport to catch his plane. He was running late, so he started to jog up the escalator. When he got closer to the top, the steps of the escalator got smaller, and being in a rush, he tried to jump over the little step only to fall flat on his face. He related his experience to that of the football season. In the beginning, you take big steps. As you get closer to the end of the season, big steps become small steps, and if you skip over them, you will fall back."

This story is a good reminder to all of us to pay attention to the little things, so you can make changes when your teen goes in the wrong direction. When you email, text, and scroll through social media while you are with your kids, you are skipping the little steps of observing, listening, and watching what is going on in their lives. It's those little steps that lead to the big payoff. In that off moment of observation, you may detect a clue to something you never expected. It's the moments when they are not performing that tell the real story. Here are some tips to be a better observer.

Stop Scrolling

When you are with your kids—especially on weekends—don't waste precious time on social media. Be engaged in the moment, not obsessed with taking the perfect selfie or making a story on Snapchat. No one cares how #blessed you are to be a #soccermomwhocarries #cleats and brings #snacks. If you are single, it's not the time to be texting your new girlfriend or boyfriend. When you are with your child, focus on them. This time is fleeting, and you will never get it back.

Schedule Time with Your Teen

As your teenagers get older, they spend less time with you and more time with their peers. Make a point to schedule something together—whether it's having a meal, doing the grocery shopping, or going for a run. Anything to get that face-to-face time.

Don't Give Up

When your teen slams the door and hibernates in their bedroom, it's easy to assume they don't want or need you. But that's not always true. Knock on the door and make up an excuse to go in and talk.

Don't Miss Their Performances

Whether it's a recital, an art show, a school play, or varsity football, showing up means everything to them. They'll remember when you don't.

Teach Them to Be Clutch Players

A clutch player musters up the strength, the focus, and whatever else it takes to perform at the highest level when it means the most. It's easy to get nervous and choke when the stakes are the highest. In football, one of the biggest differences between a winning team and a championship team is how they react under pressure. Former placekicker Lawrence Tynes described how he was able to perform under great pressure:

> "I never got caught up in the end result; just the process. Naturally, there are butterflies: But I think you are nervous only if you are unprepared. The only thing you can take with you is your routine. If you take care of your routine, your routine will take care of you. In that position, you have to be focused for three and a half hours. You always have to be on the ready."

Troy Aikman explained how he was able to perform under intense pressure during his football career.

> "When the stakes have been the highest, it's allowed me to get more focused. The bigger the moment, the more attention is brought to it. I get more locked in and raise my performance. It's something I'm really proud of."

Performing under pressure is tough for teenagers, and they are constantly in that scenario. Whether it's an exam, a big game, a performance or speech, learning to be a clutch player in the fourth quarter is a skill they must master. You can help them with these suggestions.

Visualize

When your teens say, "I can't," remind them of when they *did*! Go over what it sounded like, what it looked like, and what it felt like. This exercise boosts confidence and brings positivity to the situation.

James Dunning Jr., a parent coach for Pop Warner, AAU baseball, and AAA hockey, said,

> "In coaching, you have to set up a vision of success. I would tell the kids I coached, 'You have to envision yourself throwing a strike, throwing a good pass, catching the ball . . .'"

Be in the Moment

Lawrence Tynes had one job—to kick a field goal. If he missed, it could cost his team the game and no one would ever forget it. While he knew he could never control the end result, what he could control was his preparation. Focus on the journey, not the destination. If your child is struggling with an English paper, discuss the themes that relate to their life and make it an interesting exercise rather than rushing through it just to be done.

Do a Walk-Through

Saturday is walk-through day in the NFL. It allows everyone to make adjustments without worrying about emotions, and it enables them to get prepared for whatever comes at them. Doing walk-throughs at home can be helpful for your teenagers, too. If your daughter has an ice-skating competition, go over what to do if she falls, if she forgets her choreography, if the music does not play, or if the judges are looking down instead of at her. The walk-through lays the foundation for a plan of action before the actual scenarios arise. When your teenager has already encountered a situation once (even in their mind), it gives them the ability to make the right choice on the fly.

Focus

The distractions of cell phones and social media could destroy the focus of Albert Einstein. Help your teens by removing distractions from their room such as cell phones, iPads, and laptops if they don't need the Internet. If they need the Web for research, be sure they are not getting pinged on their computers during study time. Have them work at a desk with good light—not in a room with the TV blasting. If they become accustomed to working in a proper setting, they'll carry over that habit into college and beyond.

The Sack

There will always be times when the world tries to rattle your quarterback. Sometimes, they will even get sacked. To get your teen back on the field for the second half and ready to run with the ball, help them build their confidence, and make them believe they can be successful despite a setback or a failure.

Troy Aikman explained how his football training helped him as a parent:

> "From my training as a quarterback and my under-standing that perfection doesn't exist, I know that mistakes happen. You do the best you can, and you try to teach that and coach that."

It's hard to watch our kids when they are struggling or suffering defeat. It hurts us—sometimes even more than it hurts them.

Here are some coach parenting techniques to help them bounce back when it seems like the game has gotten away from them.

Celebrate the Positives

When your teen is feeling down, build them up as best you can and show them how they can be proactive to remedy a situation. For example, if your son is rejected by the first girl he ever really liked, you know his heartbreak will pass, but you still want to help. While you can't fix his broken heart, you can point out how handsome he is, or all the girls who like him that he is not interested in, or just his great sense of humor. Telling him he screwed up the relationship because he texted her nonstop and overdid it on the gifts is not what he needs to hear in that moment. When he's feeling better and has moved on, you can talk to him about giving girls some space and taking his time before declaring his love.

Protect the Team

Jedd Fisch mentioned a motto he learned when he worked for the Seattle Seahawks:

> "When I worked for [head coach] Pete Carroll, one of his mottoes was 'Protect the team.' This means you understand you represent all of us in your behaviors. When you go out and make a bad decision, you are making a bad decision that reflects us all."

Your family is your team and you must protect them whenever possible. While you recognize your child's areas of weakness or something they may have done wrong, you coach them how to make the changes in private. Coach Billick advised,

> "Publicly, you have to support the player as you see the coaches do. But privately, you take a different path. You support kids publicly, but when you go home, you sit down and get them to recognize there is an accountability for their actions."

A true coach parent never humiliates, shames, or embarrasses their teen in front of friends, or makes their teen the butt of their jokes. This not only leads to conflict in the home—it can eat away at or destroy your child's self-esteem. You will never fix a behavior through humiliation. If you have a tendency to embarrass your kids when they mess up, this is the time for *you* to make a halftime adjustment. Would you like to be made fun of at work by all your colleagues for an embarrassing mistake? Would you want them posting a picture of you as stupidest employee of the week? That would humiliate you and make you want to quit your job. Give your kids the same courtesy at home that you would like from your coworkers at the office.

Don't Get Distracted by What Others Are Doing

Of course, you have to be competitive, but don't assume other families have it all figured out. It would be nice if your daughter could play violin like your sister's kid or your son could get straight As without studying like the twins who live next door. But your child has other strengths. I have a friend who always tells me about her overachieving children who are the captains of every club, the top of every class, and probably saving the world right now. Every time we speak, I feel like a complete failure as a parent. But the truth is, I have to focus on helping my children be the best *they* can be so they can compete in their area of strength. This will give them *their* edge in life and boost their confidence.

When the Going Gets Tough, the Coach Gets Going

Hall of Famer and former Oakland Raiders defensive end Howie Long has two sons who play in the NFL and one son who works for the Oakland Raiders. As a dad and a former player, he often gives his kids pointers. When his son Chris was going through a rough patch playing for the Rams, Howie gave him great advice:

> "Chris played for the Rams for eight years. They averaged four and a half wins a year. There were Sunday nights where I ran out of ways to spin it. But my message was regardless of what happens around you—the score, the record—your first play should look like your eightieth play. Regardless of what's happening, you *play*."

Howie Long's approach is the embodiment of coach parenting. Yes, he knew Chris was having a rough time, but his advice to be a professional and do his best is what coach parents teach their children. Your kids will have momentum swings in life. They will have bad teachers, unfair coaches, jobs they don't like, and relationships that don't work out. The coach parent helps them develop the mental toughness to go up against tough competitors, handle rejection, and tough it out in a less than ideal situation.

You teach them to persevere through the hard times and still give it their all no matter how defeated they feel. This work ethic and ability to make adjustments when things do not go their way will be what makes them strong and helps them through the ups and downs of life. Then, when they do get the ball, they will recognize the opportunity, know exactly what to do, and execute a play to run it straight into the end zone!

Chapter 6

PERSONAL FOUL

I n professional football, when a player uses unnecessary roughness like pulling on an opponent's face mask to turn his head or hitting the opponent after the end of a play, he can incur a personal foul resulting in a fifteen-yard penalty. Unsportsmanlike conduct such as taunting or fighting with the opponent, overdoing the celebration after the touchdown, or yelling at an official can also result in the same penalty. Although the penalty is called on one player, the whole team pays the price. Sometimes, that fifteen yards can cost the team the game.

While coaches can forgive a mistake, personal fouls are tougher to take because they are preventable. Coach Jim Harbaugh explained how he might handle a player incurring personal fouls.

> "Maybe, take the ball in your hand and walk fifteen yards back the other way and say, 'That's how much you cost us this time. Also, think about what that personal foul *might* have cost us. If we tossed it out to the running back who ran

fifty yards for a touchdown, on the other side of the field, it cost us fifty yards, and the touchdown got negated by your foul, your mistake.' There are eleven players, eleven different opportunities to make a play successful. One player that gets a personal foul will negate the efforts of the other ten players."

When it comes to teenagers, there are lots of personal fouls, and often your family pays the price. Let's say your daughter, who only has a learner's permit and is not allowed to drive without an adult, takes the family car without permission. She decides to drive to the mall and ends up hitting another car. She may suffer by losing her permit, but it's your insurance premiums that go up. If you follow Coach Harbaugh's approach, you make your daughter understand that she is not the only one affected by her actions. By deducting her allowance money or making her work to help pay for the damage done to the other car, you are making her walk the fifteen yards on the field so she feels the consequences of her behavior.

Why Does the Player Run the Wrong Route?

As parents, it's important to recognize what's going on in our teenagers' minds and bodies so we can try to help them steer clear of avoidable mistakes. A post on the Harvard Medical School's Health Blog entitled "The Adolescent Brain: Beyond Raging Hormones" states some research about teenagers' brains and explains why our kids do things that we think they seem smart enough to avoid:

"Adolescents, compared to adults, find it more difficult to interrupt an action under way (stop speeding); to think before acting (learn how deep the water is before you dive); and even to choose between safer and riskier alternatives. It is easy for them to say that they would not get into a car with a drunk driver, but more difficult to turn down the invitation in practice. Adolescents' judgment can be overwhelmed by the urge for new experiences, thrill-seeking, and sexual and aggressive impulses. They sometimes seem driven to seek experiences that produce strong feelings and sensations."

The reality is every teen uses poor judgment at some point. They are all going to make mistakes, most of which can be corrected. However, getting into a car after drinking, having sex without protection, or taking Molly at a party can change the course of your teen's life—forever. The coach parent tries to anticipate these types of life-altering mistakes before they happen and does their best to help a teen who has made a bad choice that has led to harsh consequences.

In the news, we frequently hear about talented football players who have a bright career on the field but who make poor decisions off the field and end up destroying their future. They often blame their teammates, their coaches—everyone but themselves. Coach Zimmer has seen this with players, but he works at trying to keep them on the right path.

"Sometimes, I get a player who is very talented, but he continually is his own worst enemy. I sit down with him and I tell him, 'What will happen to you is you will get cut, and someone else will pick you up. And then you'll get cut again. Then, you may get one more chance, but in two years you'll say, "What happened to my career?" You are lucky that I will continue to push you until you figure this out.' I try to talk to them about what they can become and what's holding them back."

Coach Vermeil advised that in order to get your kids to listen to you and take responsibility for their actions, they need to trust that you truly have their best interests at heart:

"Caring is not just being nice. You need to care enough to get all over them and drive them. If they know you care, they will accept it, and it will deepen their respect for you. It is the first step in developing trust."

From the advice of Coach Zimmer and Coach Vermeil, we learn three important lessons.

· **Stay on them.**
If your teenager is constantly getting in trouble, do not give up. You can't *wish* them to stay on a good path. You have to *put* them there and monitor them closely.

· **Show you care.**
Setting limits and enforcing discipline by pushing them, when need be, and giving them consequences for negative actions is how you care for them. Like Coach Vermeil said, caring is not just about being nice.

- **Be trustworthy.**

To be credible, your teen needs to feel you are in their court and everything you are doing is to help them achieve, improve, and be their best.

Anger Management

All parents know that being moody, angry, aggressive, and emotional is part of normal teenage development. However, if these feelings are not properly harnessed, they can lead to serious consequences. Often, teens feel their anger is an excuse to hurt someone either physically or emotionally, and without accountability. Many parents will chalk emotional outbursts up to teenage angst, but uncontrolled anger can get kids expelled from school, in trouble with the law, and physically injured. Coach Billick cautioned against making excuses for bad behavior.

> "We dismiss a lot of things as 'passionate' as if that's okay. We enable kids that way. Road rage is 'passionate,' but it's not okay. The challenge with kids is for them to understand that passion is important, but it has to be regulated and have a purpose. Passion without purpose is uncontrolled rage. You have to show them how counterproductive it is. When a player lets his emotions get the better of him, the coach has to get him to recognize how he is hurting the team."

Parents of aggressive teenagers have to demonstrate to their teens how their actions not only hurt them, but can hurt the family. It's expensive to bail someone out of jail and hire a lawyer to defend them. If a friend comes over and gets in a physical altercation and is seriously injured, a family can be sued and lose everything. A brawl gone bad can cost a family their reputation and in some cases their livelihood. One bad punch could knock someone to the ground and cause serious injury.

However, when teenagers are in the heat of the moment, they are not always thinking clearly. Parents of aggressive kids need to find ways to help them.

Identify Triggers

If you are seeing a lot of anger in your teen, note when it happens and what causes it. Here are some common triggers and tips to follow:

Hunger

Tip 1
Don't ask teens to do anything until they have eaten.

Tip 2
Skipping meals and poor nutrition can lead to moodiness and anger. Be sure your teen is on a schedule of eating regularly.

Tip 3
Keep lots of food in the house to warm up if you're not home, so your children can eat when they need to.

Energy Drinks

Tara Parker-Pope discusses these drinks in her article in *The New York Times* entitled "Taste for Quick Boost Tied to Taste for Risk." She writes,

> "The Journal of American College Health *published a report on the link between energy drinks, athletics, and risky behavior. The study's author, Kathleen Miller, an addiction researcher at the University of Buffalo, says it suggests that high consumption of energy drinks is associated with 'toxic jock' behavior, a constellation of risky and aggressive behaviors including unprotected sex, substance abuse, and violence . . .*"

Energy drinks contain anywhere from 100 to 400 milligrams of caffeine in a twelve-ounce serving. Compare that to a typical cola, which has 34 milligrams. Their sweet taste combined with the cold temperature may induce teens to consume a larger amount in a short time span. With this in mind, it's best not to keep energy drinks in the house. If your kids are dependent on them, work to eliminate these drinks from their diet and opt for more sleep to feel energized.

Lack of Sleep

While teenagers need nine hours of sleep a night, most tend to get fewer than that. Homework, sports, part-time jobs, online activities, and being on their phones all night account for part of this. Poor sleep habits can lead to moodiness, poor performance in school, and often anger. Here are some tips to make sure your kids are getting the sleep they need.

Tip 1
If your teens nap after school, limit the nap to forty-five minutes.

Tip 2
No caffeine after 3:00 p.m.

Tip 3
Have a set time each night when they need to power down.

Tip 4
Do not allow them to do homework in bed. Bed is for sleeping; the desk is for working. Doing homework in bed confuses the two and generally leads to less productivity and poor sleep habits.

Frustration

The teenage years are a time of struggle for many—probably most—young adults. Between their changing bodies, the insecurities, and the insatiable desire for popularity, life can be quite frustrating. The tips below will help your teenagers better cope through these tough years.

Tip 1
Look Good, Feel Great
Help them feel confident in their looks by having their acne treated by a dermatologist. Check into Invisalign® clear aligners instead of metal braces and contact lenses

instead of glasses. Looking their best is always a confi-dence booster.

Tip 2
Boost Academic Performance
If they struggle in school, be sure they are in the right classes—those where they can succeed. They should not be in advanced classes if they don't have the ability to do the work. If they need extra help, seek out a peer tutor or after-school help. A few months of tutoring can make the difference in a child's ability to grasp the concepts and move forward on their own.

Tip 3
Get Moving
Get them physically active every day. If they are not gifted in competitive sports, they can go for a run, take a dance class, swim, or do martial arts. If they don't want to be in a social situation for exercise, get them a video game where they can move to music they like. It's fun and it's private.

Being Bullied
Being bullied is a common problem for teenagers, especially on social media. It's hard to prevent, but there are a few things your teen can do to avoid having it occur in the first place.

Tip 1
Think Before Posting
Tell your teen to think before posting those selfies to social media, especially the ones in bathing suits or barely-there outfits. If they don't post pictures, there is less for bullies to make fun of.

Tip 2
Do Not Respond
If your teens are bullied online, tell them not to respond and to let you know immediately. Often, online bullies move on when they don't get the desired response from their designated victims.

Tip 3
Say Something
If your child is being bullied at school, the school should be informed right away. Help them seek out a group of like-minded teens so that they feel supported during the school day. If the bullying gets severe, try to get the school to put an end to it. If that does not work, seek an alternative school setting if that is at all possible.

Stop the Blame Game

If you ever listen to teenagers, nothing is ever their fault. They got a bad grade because the teacher is unfair. They did not get minutes in the game because the coach hates them. Even Coach Shanahan experienced this with his kids when they were growing up.

"When my son and my daughter would complain about a teacher, I would say, 'Well, how is that relevant? That's what life is. Your job is, you're a student, and they have the final say, so how you deal with these people determines your success. You are going to deal with a lot of people who are not right. But then, when you are the boss, you will know what *not* to do. You will learn that there are a lot of people out there who aren't fair.'"

Here is where coach parenting differs from the helicopter parenting we see today. The coach parent does not accept excuses from their children. Instead, you teach your child they must work their hardest in a class where they do not like the teacher and power through a practice even though they disagree with the coach's plays. One day, they will have a boss they don't like or agree with, but they will have to do their job or get fired. This is a valuable lesson that will prepare your teens for the real-world experiences that are just around the corner.

How to Stop the Excuses

- **Don't join the pity party.**

Teens love to complain how the world is against them because in their mind, it absolves them of responsibility for wrongdoing or failure. Hold them accountable for their actions and help them identify where they went wrong, what they could have done better, and how to avoid the pitfall in the future.

Continued

> · **Trust the teacher/coach/authority figure.**
> Teaching teenagers is a difficult job, and often teachers and coaches teach because it's their passion. In most cases, the coach parent should give the benefit of the doubt to the authority figure; not their child. While no parent wants to believe their kid is being manipulative, lazy, or stretching the truth, an adult's perspective is usually more accurate than that of a teenager.

Make It Right

Your teenagers are going to say the wrong thing, post the inappropriate picture, and break your rules from time to time. It's how they own up to their mistakes that counts the most. Coach John Harbaugh and I discussed the best course of action when you make a mistake or do the wrong thing.

> "Do right or make it right. If you break a rule, you have to make it right and respond, because then it's done and gone and you don't have to look back. We are *all* going to make mistakes. They want to see what you do *after* you screw up. It doesn't mean you can't disagree with a call. But sometimes you cross a line and you have to say to the ref, 'I'm sorry. I should not have said that.'"

When your kids make a mistake, teach them to fix it by admitting to it, saying they were wrong, and apologizing or whatever is appropriate to the situation. Then, they can learn from it and keep pushing forward.

Control Your Emotions

It's easy to have a knee-jerk reaction when your child does something wrong and say things out of emotion. But an emotional outburst is not always the best way to talk to your kids, especially when they screw up. Most kids know when they did something wrong. Tiki Barber feels it's important to stay in control of your feelings and emotions, so you say what you mean and mean what you say.

> "I was at the Super Bowl the year Mike Tomlin won. He was calm, steady, and in the moment—and not overwhelmed. When I asked him, 'Why are you so calm?' he said, 'I like to control my emotions because I like to see things with clarity.' From him, I learned to try to stay calm and not let emotion or haste make me say something."

When we get emotional, we say and do things we don't mean. No matter what your child has done, gain your composure before confronting the situation. Teens can be infuriating, but yelling and screaming when they mess up often gets met with more yelling and screaming. Take a moment and think about what you want to say, how you want to say it, and your desired outcome.

Cool It Down

If you want to defuse your teen's anger, you need to defuse yours first—especially if your child is watching. Kids learn by observation. The Childhood Domestic Violence Association cites, "Children of domestic violence are three times more likely to repeat the cycle in adulthood, as growing up with domestic violence is the most significant predictor of whether or not someone will be engaged in domestic violence later in life."

For men: Be mindful not to yell, use profanity, or speak in an abusive way to women—especially to your child's mother, grandmother, or sisters. When a boy observes a man treat women in that manner, he learns to do the same.

For women: Treat the men in your house respectfully. Avoid putting down or belittling your teen's father.

No matter how you feel about your child's father or mother, that person is still their parent. We love our parents and don't wish to think poorly of them. Whatever issues you have with the mother or father of your child should not be shared with your children. It's a burden they should not have to take on.

Don't Get Physical

You would not be human if you did not want to physically grab your teenager when they get you to that breaking point. But violence teaches violence. Never hit your teenager *even* if you were hit when you were a kid. You *can't* "beat some sense" into someone. It escalates the situation and could turn dangerous for everyone involved. Violence is not an acceptable form of solving problems. It just shows your child that you are completely out of control. Disciplining teenagers in a physical way teaches them violence is okay. This could lead to them being violent with others outside the home.

Channel the Aggressive Energy

Teenagers have boundless energy (except in the morning when they need to get up for school). The best way to deal with the moodiness and lethargy is to get those endorphins going and tire them out. They need exercise—and a lot of it. Here are a few ways to get them to work up a sweat.

Sports

Team sports are not for everyone, and many kids can't play varsity. If your kids are on a team, that's great—it will be easier for you and them. But if they are not good enough or not inclined to play on a team, help them find a sport they can do outside of school. Running, cross-country skiing, swimming, tennis, and squash are examples of sports they can do at their own pace. Good habits and new friends can also be a result of getting out and trying something new. Network with other parents to find out what their kids are doing.

Martial Arts/Boxing

Unlike team sports, everybody can do martial arts. It's a wonderful way for teens to learn to control their aggressive energy and calm their minds. It also gives them an outlet to fight in a controlled setting while teaching them discipline and respect for their instructors and other people. Boxing is perfect for that teen, boy or girl, who has a lot of pent-up anger and frustration.

Performing Arts

People involved in the performing arts often bond over the love of their art form. If your teen doesn't fit into a clique or can't find that perfect peer group, put them in an acting class where they can explore their feelings and emotions. Dancing, singing, acting, and playing an instrument are all outlets for self-expression that can help with feelings of depression and loneliness. Even something as simple as going to a hip-hop class can get the endorphins flowing and lift their spirits.

Weight Lifting

A weight-lifting program for your teen at a local Y or recreational center can offer supervised strength training. Regardless of their abilities in other sports, teenagers may find the weight room to be the perfect place to get strong, get fit, and burn energy.

Part-Time Jobs

Manual labor is a great way for kids to make money after school or on the weekends while they let off some steam and build strength at the same time. They can shovel snow, rake leaves, take out a neighbor's garbage, babysit, walk a neighbor's dog, or do yard work.

Run/Walk/Bike for a Cause

Every week in most communities, there is a run for some sort of charity. Encourage your kids to do community service by running, walking, or biking for a good cause. Being around people who choose to help others can also bring your kids into contact with good role models. Even better, help your teenager to organize a run/walk/climb for a cause that has affected their life.

Know When to Pull Them Off the Field

Anger and aggressive behavior are habit-forming and need to be dealt with at a young age. If your teen is physically aggressive at home toward parents or siblings, or is cruel to animals, you have an issue that is bigger than you. These behaviors may be indicative of a psychological problem that should be addressed as soon as possible.

If your teen is making your home physically unsafe, you may need to look for residential programs where the child can live and go to school in a place that can provide help. Residential programs are highly structured and have the staff to assist students who need this support. These programs can be costly, but often your local department of education can help you find affordable options. In some states, the cost may even be reimbursed by a government program. Remember, in a residential program, you have control and can pull your child out whenever it is appropriate. Once they get in trouble with the law, your options are limited.

Who Is in Your Teen's Huddle?

Whether the issues involved are drinking, drugs, sex, or car surfing down your street, you have to be vigilant about who your teen chooses as friends. If you have ever heard the expression "Birds of a feather flock together," there is actually a reason for this. According to Dr. Unterberg,

"Destructive aggression usually occurs because people believe they know and have a very strong belief about how things should be, how a woman should be, how a friend should be. They have real problems if someone says no or does not agree with them. They think they are right and have *the* truth. They become enraged if the other person does not agree and see it the same way. So they join others who share in their beliefs."

If your daughter likes to make fun of people, she will surround herself with others who like to do that too. Her friends are reinforcing a belief that she may not even realize she has. If someone tells her this is wrong, she may lash out at them for disagreeing with her and not enabling her belief system. If your son thinks it's cool to degrade women, chances are his friends think and do the same. So, how does the coach parent encourage a good huddle or break up a bad one?

Get to Know the Families

Invite your kids' friends and their families to your home for a barbecue or to watch a game. I try to attend a mom's night out whenever I can so I can stay in contact with the moms of my kids' friends. Other parents are great sources of information on what's going on in your teen's extended group.

Have Your Kids Draw Their Own Conclusions

Casually ask your kids about their friendships. Start with a positive such as, "You're on such a great track. Are your friends doing well in school too? Why did your friend get in trouble last week? Do you think he/she might bring you down with them?" You may have to dig a little for the information you're looking for, but you will find they like having someone to confide in about what their friends are doing.

Break It Up

If your teenagers are in the wrong crowd and associating with kids who are using drugs or alcohol, or participating in illegal activities, the peer pressure and negative influence is going to be strong. Pulling them out of that group will be tough. Sometimes, when a teenager is attracted to these elements, there is something deeper going on. If they have gone through something troubling such as a move, a divorce, or a death, they could be seeking a way to self-soothe. But often, they just want to be cool, and the "cool kids" in their eyes are also the ones who are vandalizing cars.

While psychotherapy can be helpful if they have been through a trauma, it's a long process and may take some time to effect change. If you are involved in a faith-based group, seek out the help of a chaplain who works with teenagers. Sometimes kids who are in a bad crowd benefit from the emotional and spiritual

Continued

guidance of a counselor grounded in faith. If there is a teacher, a coach, or an adult they respect, ask them to help you speak to your child.

Most important, try to get your teenager to talk to you about their friends. Walk through the possible scenarios with them of what their future could be if they stay in the wrong crowd.

No Hard Feelings

When tempers flare up, it's easy for everyone to start slamming doors and cutting off communication with one another. You may, unintentionally, say something hurtful to your child, and the resentment starts to brew. But the coach parent always reaches out to their teenager with love as soon as possible. Coach Billick talked about how a good coach defuses anger, whether it's with a child or a player.

"You can't relinquish your parenting obligation when your kids are self-destructive: You intercede. It's tough for them to hear. If all you do is lay down rules, you may be right—but at some point, they are going to resent the messenger. They need to have the ability to voice their opinions. For example, in a game, it gets quite heated. You don't have time to collect a player and throw that warm fuzzy arm around him and say, 'That is not how I want you do it.' You have time constraints, so you may say, 'Damn it. You did it wrong.' So, you have to come back later. With Bill Walsh [late head coach of the San Francisco 49ers], this would happen a lot. He would be correcting a player, and he would be public about it. You have to circle back around at dinner that night and say, 'Look, you know why I did what I did. If you were me, what could I have done better?'"

Unfortunately, there will always be times when you and your teenager are going to butt heads. It's part of the growing-up process, and it helps them pull away so they can become independent. But it's up to the coach parent to ensure there are no bad feelings—no matter how big a blowup you had with your child. We have a rule in our home: No one goes to bed angry. We work it out. If you have had an issue with your teenager, and they have not come on their own to you to apologize, you need to go to them and start the healing process once emotions have cooled down. You can do this in four simple steps.

1. **Initiate the conversation.**

   When the dust has settled after the blowup, go talk to your teenager. Ask how they are feeling and what needs to happen next to remedy the situation. This may take some time, so be patient.

2. **Discuss your role in the altercation.**

   Discuss your motives and the way you handled the situation. Don't be afraid to admit that perhaps you could have said what you said in a better way

*or at a better time. Ask them what they would
have done in your shoes. This can yield some interesting insights.*

3. **Validate your teenager.**

   *Tell them you understand why they feel as they do
   and why they got upset with you. Let them know
   you might have been upset, too, if you had been in
   their position.*

4. **Hug them.**

   *Tell them that you love them and that you hope the
   two of you can move past the incident. A hug, a kiss,
   an "I love you," and a good night's sleep usually do
   the trick.*

The adolescent years are a struggle for every parent. Your
kids are going to act without thinking and make mistakes
that were preventable if only they had not been so impulsive.
While the coach parent tries to prevent them from going
down the wrong path, sometimes it happens faster than you
think, and you could be faced with difficult decisions. But
your job is not to judge them or feel sorry for yourself. Help
them through the turmoil and know when you can't do it
alone. Remember, a head coach of a football team has the
support of position coaches, chaplains, doctors, and psychia-
trists to help them navigate the issues that come up for each
player. When faced with trouble with your teen, seek the
counsel of anyone who will listen. Never give up on your
child. There is always another game to be played.

Chapter 7

...

CYBER BOWL

O ur teenagers are the first generation to grow up in a digital world where sharing life's every moment is normal and even expected. For football players, like for our children, social media is a double-edged sword. They can use it to promote themselves, their causes, and their team, and feel the love of their fans. But, one poorly thought-out post or a mistake on the field can garner the wrath of their fan base and even cost them endorsement deals.

Our teenagers are encountering the same types of ups and downs as these athletes, but among their peer group. They actually know most of the people writing the comments, which can make those remarks all the more hurtful to their already fragile self-esteem. As parents, we know what is appropriate in what setting. But in our kids' world, everything is for public consumption. Their sense of boundaries and privacy is different. Bob Costas spoke with me about the effects social media is having on our youth.

"It has changed where personal, family, and team boundaries are. Often, players will post whatever they think is interesting, not realizing it could be detrimental to their team. It used to be clear when a conversation was just at the dinner table as opposed to a public gathering, or an online discussion. Those are all different venues, and what's appropriate at home may not be suitable in other contexts. As a result, many young people have an unclear sense of their own boundaries. For coaches, it should not have much or any effect on how they actually coach, but still, when a drumbeat builds during a losing streak, social media goes nuts. That affects and distorts the atmosphere. You have to be aware of the distortion and either diffuse it with something funny or convince your players to either ignore it, or better yet, not participate in it at all."

When literally everyone is on social media today, how are teens supposed to understand what should and should not be posted? Even though it seems any topic is fair game, it's more important than ever to teach privacy and boundaries to our kids.

My son recently went on a school trip to a YMCA camp in the Catskill Mountains with two other schools. They had no access to cell phones, Wi-Fi, or the Internet. When they returned, my son and his friends told me how relaxing it was to have two days free from posting, Snapchatting, or texting. They did not have to stop every minute to take pictures of their dinner or selfies in their bunk. No one worried they were being secretly filmed while they were sleeping. The fact that they were happy to be away from it all shows us what a high state of anxiety and distraction our kids live in as a result of social media.

Coach Billick talked about how social media has changed the world of football coaching just as it has altered the world of parenting.

> "For young coaches, it's the number one challenge and difficulty, because everything about our society has basically become about *me*. Everybody is glorifying themselves and their existence on social media, and that cuts at the heart of *team*, which is about *we* rather than *I*."

We can't beat social media because it's here to stay. Instead, we have to join it and try to transform it from a negative to a positive in our teens' lives.

Coach Parenting Social Media Rules

- If you don't have something nice to post, don't post it.

- If you are hesitant to post it, you probably shouldn't.

- Before posting a picture, or writing a comment, ask yourself how you would feel if everyone in your school saw it.

Brand *ME* and Privacy

Everybody is now a "brand" with a social media persona. For a young football player, becoming a social media sensation is enticing. Who doesn't want to be an Instagram darling with followers hanging on your every post? But while the players may be experts in football, the incorrectly worded tweet or the inappropriate post can mean serious trouble for them and hurt their brand.

As a parent of two teenagers, I worry every day about what they are posting and how it could affect their future. This is where the parenting and the coaching come to the forefront. You can't assume your teenagers have the same sense of privacy you do. They need to be coached on the importance of privacy to protect them, the family, and even their "brand."

Big Brother Should Not Be in Your Home

People are watching and recording all the time. Even the comings and goings in your home—which should be a place of privacy—are being recorded—by your own security cameras or by those at the nearby traffic light, the grocery store parking lot, or on someone's drone. While the outside cameras are beyond your jurisdiction, the handheld electronic devices are in your control. No one in your home should worry that a private meltdown at home over a bad breakup or a failed test is being secretly live-streamed on Facebook. Coach John Harbaugh's take on privacy and not embarrassing one another comes from the late Coach Vince Lombardi, who lived in a time before social media.

> "Coach Lombardi said, 'What you see here, what
> you say here, what you hear here, let it stay here,
> when you leave here. This is family.'"

I love this quote because it embodies what home should be—a place of comfort, safety, and security. You may have seen a parent "punishing" their teen's bad behavior by writing them open letters on Facebook that go viral or secretly videotaping them talking back and posting it to Twitter. This public shaming is all over the morning news shows every week—along with the proud parents who bask in the glory of their fame at the expense of their child. This is *not* coach parenting! It's selfish, look-at-me-I-need-attention-and-validation parenting, and it destroys all trust between parent and child.

Block the Opponent

Kids are growing up in a time where everything they say can be recorded and posted to the Internet. That's why they need to be extra careful in public or at a party with friends. If they are filmed smoking from a bong, drinking alcohol, hooking up with an intoxicated girl or boy, or vandalizing property, they could face serious consequences which can, at best, cause them embarrassment and, at worst, get them in trouble with the law and hinder future opportunities such as college acceptances and scholarships.

During the first round of the 2016 NFL draft, left tackle Laremy Tunsil was likely to be a top-five draft pick, but his position fell to number thirteen when someone posted a picture of him smoking marijuana wearing a gas mask. Of course, there was no date on the picture, and it was not clear who posted it, but the result of this picture cost Tunsil millions of dollars. Someone had it in for Tunsil and wanted to hurt him. Coach Mariucci was covering the draft when that happened and told me how it played out.

> "We were at the draft. During the show on my colleague's phone, here comes a picture of Tunsil with a gas mask smoking marijuana, and he is about to get drafted! There is a lot of money at stake. All of a sudden, his draft status began to fall."

Tunsil was eventually drafted, but the dollars were not what they could have been had he not suffered the backlash of those photos. This story shows parents just how powerful a force social media can be in our kids' lives. It's the opponent they do not see coming for them.

Social Media Guidelines for the Coach Parent

Sharing is not always caring.
When in doubt, do not post a picture of your teen without their permission for both the picture and the caption.

Kids create a persona and a unique brand of their own through their social media posts. The naked baby in the bathtub picture you feel compelled to post on Throwback Thursday may be extremely embarrassing to your kids and contrary to the image they have so carefully constructed. Remember, nothing is ever truly deleted online. A screenshot can be shared multiple times.

Learn to be social media savvy.
It is your job to use, understand, and know your way around a group chat, Snapchat, and Instagram.

The days of the parent who "doesn't know how" to use social media because they don't like it are over. You can't teach your teen what is appropriate to post or not to post if you are not in that world. Ask them to show you what apps they are on and have them teach you how to use them. Also, tell them you would like to follow their accounts, not to spy on them, but just to make sure they are not posting something that could jeopardize their future chances of getting into college or getting a job. If you do not like a post, you can text them to take it down.

Be an example.
Before you post anything, think of how your posts will be perceived by your children.

I see parents posting provocative selfies, using profanity, holding up the middle finger, and bragging about drunken escapades on social media all the time. Most of them are good parents who just don't stop to think about the implications of their posts. They believe because it's on Facebook, it's somehow private amongst their friends. But NOTHING IS PRIVATE online. Your kids can and will see your posts and will think if you post it, they should too.

Be Social Media Sensitive to Your Teen

- Don't post anything about your teen without their permission.

- Don't use social media as a disciplinary tool or humiliate them publicly to make a point.

- Don't tag your teens in your posts without their permission.

- Don't comment on your teen's posts.

- Do not send out friend requests to your teen's friends without your child's knowledge.

- If you do follow their friends, do not comment on their posts.

- Don't post your exploits (i.e., pictures of you drinking and partying).

- Don't post anything school-related on social media unless it is for safety reasons.

- Don't post sexualized images or quotes.

- Don't have private conversations with your teens over social media.

Social Media Guidelines for Teens

Take away the ball.

Social media and online chatting can be a time-suck, leaving little time for much else. In the settings of your teenager's phone, look together at how much time they spend talking, texting, and using apps. Many of these hours are spent late at night when they should be sleeping. Charging their electronics outside of their room is a good way to eliminate the distraction so they can get a restful night's sleep without the pinging!

Rethink the play.
While it may seem like celebrities are getting attention for their *spontaneous* selfies in their underwear, in reality, many of those pictures are lit and shot by professional photographers. For actors and reality stars, being in their briefs is how they get more work. When your teen tries to emulate these shots, it can often be harmful to their future. If your teenager is posting provocative pictures, discuss what they are putting out there and why they are doing it. Remember, their future boss and the office of college admissions will likely see what they post.

Think before you snap.
Teach your teens to wait sixty seconds before posting a picture or video. It's in their possession before they put it out there. Once it's gone, it can take on a life of its own and portray them in a way they did not intend. When in doubt, call a time-out!

Take care with what you share.
Teach your kids not to share nude photos of themselves or anyone else, especially if the photo is of a minor. If they forward or share it, they can be accused of online bullying and spreading child pornography.

Consider the long game.
Your teen's social media profile should promote positive messages, their talents, and their friendships. It should not be an online magazine of them modeling their lingerie collection, their twerking abilities, or how much they can drink without getting sick.

Protect the ball.
If your teen wants their friends to know where they are, advise them to send a text. They should not post their whereabouts to social media, as this can be the

Continued

information a stalker or predator is looking for. Make sure they are aware of what apps they are using and how this information could get into the hands of people who don't need to know where your minor child is at any given time. This can be adjusted in the settings of their phone.

Use Social Media for Good

While we know all the negatives that can result from social media, if used for a good purpose, it can change the world. Coach Jim Harbaugh gave pointers on how he encourages his players to use the power of social media in a positive way.

> "Encourage them to be part of the solution, not part of the problem. Social media can be a very good thing. You can learn information. It can be fun. You can communicate with people. Peer pressure is often negative, but what if you follow the example of someone doing something really good? That can be a positive thing. You can be part of a solution by being positive on social media. You can make someone laugh or set the record straight. It doesn't have to have a negative stigma."

Coach Harbaugh's idea can give our teenagers the positive attention they crave. If you compliment someone on social media and like what they are doing, they will like you and support you back. If you are raising awareness for a cause, social media can help you spread your message and get positive feedback.

Being Positive on Social Media

- Support people doing positive things.

- Spread goodwill and support worthy causes.

- Compliment and encourage people doing good for others.

- Repost positive and inspirational stories and messages.

While you may have given up at this point and feel social media is beyond your control, try to prepare your teenagers for the landmines that lie in the cyber world. While you can't anticipate everything, help your kids learn from the mistakes of others. There are numerous examples of celebrities your children admire making both positive and negative choices on social media. Discuss the issues over dinner like a head coach would discuss film from yesterday's game. Go over what could have been done differently. Yes, our kids are often smarter than we are when it comes to the latest apps and group chats. But we know more than they do about privacy. And they crave it, but they don't know how to get it. That's why they need you to coach it!

Chapter 8

...

CAN YOU TRUST YOUR QUARTERBACK TO CALL AN AUDIBLE?

I n football, sometimes a quarterback will look at how the defense has lined up, and at the last minute he calls out a change to the play called for in the huddle. This is known as "calling an audible." If you think of your teenagers as your rookie quarterbacks, you know they are chomping at the bit to have more independence and start calling their own plays. But teenagers cannot be given that freedom right away. They need to earn the trust of the coach parent.

Troy Aikman related the experience of parenting teenagers who always want more independence to his experience as a quarterback.

> "In football, as you show an ability to execute the
> plays, you get given more. I think the same is true
> with the kids. I say to my girls, 'Here is what I
> expect, and you have to follow the rules. As I know

that I can trust you, then you get to do a little bit more.' With rookies, coaches are trying to protect the young player by not giving them too much all at once. With children, as they start to get older, as they show an ability to handle more situations, you give them a little bit more. When they show they can't, you pull back."

By the time your kids are in eighth grade, they think they are ready to take on the world. This continues into high school, when they want to hang out with the seniors, stay out all night, and not answer to anyone. But like a good football coach, you are not going to send your player out onto the field until they prove to you they can handle themselves in practice. Since the goal of coach parenting is not to go to college with your kids or have them live in your basement until they are forty, each year of high school, the coach parent works toward giving their teens more independence.

A football coach works with his quarterback to teach him the plays so he can call an audible when necessary. Coach parents work with their teenagers to teach them how to control themselves and make smart choices when there is no one there to guide them. Before you can give your team the football and tell them to run the wishbone, it's necessary to assess how responsible and trustworthy they are.

Quiz—Can You Trust Your Players?

1. **Your son has a big test tomorrow, and he is not prepared. Does he:**

   a. Try to copy off a friend.

   b. Pretend to be ill, thinking you don't know he is faking.

   c. Stay up as long as necessary to cram.

   d. Take his chances and deal with the consequences.

2. **You saw your daughter hit a parked car pulling into your driveway last night. The next morning you ask her if she knows how the dent got on the right fender. Her response is:**

   a. I have no idea.

   b. I would rather not say.

   c. I hit a parked car when pulling out of the driveway, but I will work to pay to get it fixed.

   d. It was probably my brother. He is always banging up the car.

3. **You ask your son to babysit your six-year-old nephews while you have dinner with their parents who are staying with you. You leave once the kids are asleep, and you tell your son you will be back in two hours. Does he:**

   a. Go through the parents' bag to see if they have pot.

   b. Watch TV on the couch.

   c. Start on his lab for the following week.

   d. Invite friends over without permission.

4. **Your daughter needs $10 to buy her lunch at school. You tell her to go into your wallet and take the money. You have a $20 bill and a $10 bill in your wallet. Your daughter will most likely:**

Continued

a. Take $30 and figure you won't notice.

b. Take the $20 so she won't have to ask for money tomorrow.

c. Take only the $10.

d. Ask you if it's okay if she takes the $20 in case she wants something extra.

5. **Your son finds the answers to the final exam on the floor of his classroom as he walks in. Does he:**

a. Take a picture of the answers with his phone

b. Throw them in the trash.

c. Give them to the teacher and disclose that he may have seen an answer or two.

d. Leave them on the floor; it's not his problem.

Results: Give yourself the following points for each of the answers you chose:

a. 0

b. 2

c. 5

d. 3

0–5 points—Untrustworthy! Cheats on tests, looks through someone's bag? Your teenager needs to be on a tight leash and is not ready for responsibility.

5–15 points—Your teen sees life in shades of gray, does not have a clear idea of right and wrong, and will cut corners. While somewhat trustworthy, your teen still needs some guidance and character building.

15–25 points—Trustworthy! You are lucky—your teen shows good judgment and deserves more independence.

Whether your teen scored a 5 or a 25, there are situations where the coach parent does not give their teenager the benefit of the doubt. Sometimes, peer pressure and the desire to fit in can make a good kid do bad things. Although your teen may have good judgment most of the time, their friends could have something else in mind. Just as football players practice harder when the coaches are watching, teens behave better when *you* are watching.

The Playing Field

On a college or pro football team, if the head coach is not watching, there is a position coach who has both eyes on the player. The coaches measure how much weight he is lifting, how fast he is running, and what mistakes need to be corrected. If you watch documentaries of NFL training camps, you see the players have a curfew and must follow team rules, or they will be cut. These are grown men and yet they are constantly being monitored to make sure they stay on course. So if you think your teenager does not need supervision or your focus, think again.

My sixteen-year-old son is a great kid and always very respectful of our home. I like his friends and feel quite comfortable having them over. As an example, he invited fifteen guys and girls to our home for the Super Bowl. Everybody said hello when they arrived and thank you when they left. Nobody pre-gamed or brought alcohol or pot. These are good kids. However, they are still teenagers, and there is no reason to give them an opportunity to go astray by not being present while they are in my home. The coach parent gives their teen independence as it is earned. However, there are certain situations where the playbook should stay closed. Here are some guidelines.

Do Not Take Off for the Weekend

Leaving teenagers home alone for the weekend is asking for trouble. While they may not think to have a party, a friend who hears you are away can text out an invite to everyone in school in three seconds—suddenly your home is party central.

Don't Leave Liquor Out

One night, a couple I know left a half-drunk bottle of red wine on the kitchen table. Their son's friends came over and drank that bottle and three more open bottles in the fridge. If you have teenagers, don't have alcohol in the fridge or open bottles of vodka in the freezer. Make sure your liquor cabinet has a lock on it and check it before and after your teenager's friends have gone. With clear liquors like vodka, taste it to be sure the kids didn't drink it and refill the bottle with water.

Don't Leave Cash Lying Around

You might not really know your teens' friends, and some of them could have sticky fingers. Keep your wallet and cash in a safe or a place where they cannot access it. If your teen needs money, give them the cash they need and be vigilant of cash gone missing.

Don't Leave Your Computer Open

One day, a friend of my teenager was over, and I caught him typing at my computer. He was about to post something inappropriate on my Facebook page as a joke. If your computer is not password protected, your teen or their friends can access your email and social media accounts, making it easy for them to play a prank on you. Be sure to have your computer in your bedroom where your teens' friends can't access it. For good measure, have your kids put their laptops and iPads in your bedroom while friends are over so no one can hack them, either.

Keep Your Medicine in a Lockbox

While your kids may not be interested in what's in your medicine cabinet, their friends might be. If you or anyone in your home take opiates for pain, or have anxiety, ADD, or cold medications, keep them locked up. For a drug user, your medicine cabinet is their candy store.

Lock Up Firearms

If you have guns in your home, be sure they are locked up and no one has access to them but you. Even if you regularly go to the shooting range with your kids, and they know how to safely use a gun, you don't want them or their friends to have access to a gun without your supervision.

How Your Team Can Earn Your Trust

"Don't you trust me?" said every teen on the planet to their parent at some point. Well, we want to trust you. We really do. It's just that you are fifteen and can't seem to remember how to put your clothes on a hanger, so you can see why it's a little tough on us parents. You need to *earn* our trust.

Quarterback Eli Manning started as a rookie for the New York Giants under Coach Tom Coughlin. I asked

Coach Coughlin how Manning earned his trust when he was coaching him.

> "Because of the way he is, the way he prepares, and the way he works: No complaints. 'Work me as hard as you want. Give me every opportunity to prove I can be a starting quarterback in the NFL.' Whatever test you put him through, he passed."

Coach John Harbaugh explained how it works with the Ravens:

> "Everybody wants a bigger role; they want to be able to do more. The expanding of your role is earned. If we are given a bag of money to invest, if we do well with it, we are given more of it. If we don't, we get less of it. With kids, the better you do with what you have, the more responsibility you get. In football, if you play well, then you get more playing time, you get the ball in your hands more. Too many turnovers—you are not going to play. You are handling the ball well, you are playing hard, you are playing well, you earn a bigger role."

When your teen asks you for more independence, offer some ways to earn your trust. Here are a few things your kids can do to show you they are ready for more.

1. If they make a mistake, they don't blame someone else. They own up to it!

2. Accept the consequences of their actions.

3. Communicate openly with their parents.

4. Keep their word.

5. Be truthful even if they think you won't like it.

6. Be home promptly at curfew.

7. Answer your calls and texts right away.

8. Ask for permission before borrowing the car or money.

9. Show responsibility by earning some of their own spending money.

10. Do what is asked of them *when* it is asked.

Coaching Is Caring

A football player can't play well for a head coach he doesn't trust. He needs to believe the coach is on his side and making demands to *help* him—not just to exert authority or be on a power trip. Coach Vermeil explained his philosophy on getting his players to trust him and follow his leadership.

> "My coaching staff and I always worked within this concept: 'Players don't care how much you know, until they know how much you care.' Caring is

not always as simple as it appears to be! It is *not* just a matter of being friendly—it is about caring with a purpose and moving people in the direction they need to go, even when they are reluctant, so they can move toward being the best they can be for all the right reasons."

In a family setting, teenagers are going to have conflict with their parents. To resolve it effectively, kids—like football players—need to feel their parents have their best interests at heart and are doing all they can to help them. The coach parent values their child's trust and builds it in the following ways.

Give Them a Reason to Believe

"It's much easier to do what is asked when you know why you are doing it," said Coach Zimmer. He added, "Part of my deal is getting the players to perform together as a team. When we are watching film together, I point things out and say, 'This is why you are doing this. If the nose tackle does this, then it allows our defensive end to do that.'"

If you instruct your kids to do something, give them a logical explanation of why it's necessary. For example, if your son asks why you insist he drive at the speed limit, saying "Because you just have to" doesn't inspire trust in you or a call to action by him. Instead, tell him, "If you speed and have an accident, you are more likely to get hurt or hurt someone else because the impact will be harder.

Also, if a police officer pulls you over for speeding, you will get an expensive ticket and points on your license. Too many points = suspended license!" It's always easier to follow directions when they have a purpose.

Equip Them

It's our job as parents to make the environment conducive to our children's success in every way we can. Imagine telling your son to go play tackle football but you forget to give him the pads. After one hit, he would not have much trust in your judgment. Giving kids what they need to be successful can mean any of the following:

- Giving them a quiet place to study

- Finding a tutor if they struggle in school

- If you don't have a laptop, finding a local library with public computers

- Buying or borrowing the proper gear for their sport

Show Them the Play

To get your teenagers to trust you, help them when they need assistance, and watch them follow through. Consider Coach Jim Harbaugh's example of how he coaches his players.

> "You show them how to do something—you tell them what to do, let them do it, tell them what they did wrong, what they did right, and where

they can improve. That's teaching and coaching, to me. The incentive is showing them that they can improve at something; they can be better than they were yesterday. Improvement will lead to success. That's the formula, day by day, month by month, year by year. When they see the results for themselves, they have a good feeling about what they are doing."

Let's say your kids want to cook something, even if it's simply pasta. Tell them to boil the water before putting in the pasta. Instruct them to time it according to the directions on the box and then strain it when it's done. Taste the pasta and tell them how you were impressed that it was cooked al dente—not too crunchy and not too mushy. If it's too watery, advise them to drain the water out a little more.

Once they do that, compliment them on what a great job they did. It's like if your boss not only asked you to do a project, but also showed you how to do it and once you finished it, how to make it even better. It would make you feel your boss was in your corner and believed in you—which, in turn, leads to a deeper trust.

Set Realistic Expectations

Make sure you've assessed the situation before you assign the task. Sometimes, parents expect kids to do the impossible, and then they come down hard on them when their expectations are not met. If you give your kids just two hours to clean a garage that needs five days and an army to clean, you are setting them up to disappoint you. It's difficult to trust someone who does not have a grasp on reality.

Mutuality

You are important to your teenagers and they need to feel they are important to you. It has to go both ways. If your child does everything you ask, but you are too busy to show up to their school plays or science fairs, on the phone when they want to talk, or unavailable when they need you, at some point your relationship will suffer and there will be a breakdown of trust. When trust is broken, relationships break too. Dr. Unterberg said,

> "Successful coaches develop a sense of 'mutuality' with their players. When a coach arrives, the players must feel and believe he is 'all in' for the team. The coach, in turn, must also believe that the players are doing everything they can to achieve the goal. If this occurs, *then* you have 'mutuality.' When you get away from this mutuality, you have conflict, which is why with some coaches—who are autocratic—ultimately, it doesn't work."

Dr. Unterberg's observation applies to parenting. You can't just bark orders at your children and then ignore them when they want to share something with you. When you take an interest in what interests your child, they feel validated and loved.

Since my son was little, basketball has been his passion. He plays on his high school varsity team and loves nothing more than when I reward him by taking him to an NBA game. Before he was born, I had probably been to one NBA game and was watching celebrity row more than Michael Jordan's three-pointers. (Yes, I'm dating myself here!)

Although I didn't know much about basketball, I made it my mission to know the names of every player on his favorite team, learn the game, and watch with him. When he formed an AAU team, I helped him get practice court time. I wanted him to know I was "all in."

When you take their lead, and help them pursue what they like—especially when it's not your interest—it says to them that you think what they like is important. You may even develop a new interest like I did. This type of commitment in your relationship with your teenager can bring you together in ways you never thought possible.

Pass the Torch

Super Bowl–winning coaches and Hall of Fame players make it a priority to pass the game they love on to the next generation. Howie Long talked about how much he loved coaching his sons when they were young.

> "I coached all of my boys. Coaching them was such a treat. My thought process was, *I can't help you with your chemistry, but I can teach you how the game is played and what being successful requires.* I wasn't a screamer or yeller, but my work ethic was highly driven by [my former defensive line coach] Earl Leggett. (He coached both Michael Strahan and me.) If Michael or I were to coach, we would say to ourselves, 'How did Earl do it? How did we do it under Earl?' I wanted to pass that strong

work ethic on to my boys. I felt like I could build
the foundation for how you play the game."

Coach parents teach their kids what they know. Whether
it's showing them how to fix a car, sew a dress, understand
the stock market, or bake a cake, sharing your passion with
your children is a wonderful way to bond and connect.

Interceptions

In recent years, we have seen the rise of the parent who is
so overinvolved with their child, they do whatever it takes
to shield them from failure. I knew one dad who tried to
get the drama teacher fired for not casting his daughter as
Sandy in the school production of *Grease*. He was, essen-
tially, intercepting the opportunity for his daughter to
learn to accept rejection. If you study the most successful
coaches and players in the NFL, many have been fired or
cut multiple times—which is a type of failure.

Tiki Barber told a story of how being allowed to fail
helped him in his career.

"My favorite coach was my first wrestling coach—
Steve Spangler. I was going into seventh grade,
and my brother and I wanted to play basketball.
We didn't make the team. Coach said, 'Sometimes you fail, but it doesn't mean you are not
good.' The lesson was well learned. We went out
for wrestling, and we won the district championship. It was a lesson about failure. We tend to shy
away from it. You should embrace it, because you
learn so much from failure. Nobody is perfect

in sports. No running back goes an entire career
without fumbling."

Tiki's words are an important lesson to all parents. No
player has a perfect career, and often failure (or what seems
to be failure at the time) inspires kids to work harder and
prove the naysayers wrong. Failure can also bring about
opportunities in other areas—the way not making the basketball team made Tiki available for the wrestling team.

Coach parents do *not* intercept life lessons for their kids.
Having a failure does not *make* you a failure.

Letting Them Call the Play

The goal of the coach parent is to raise responsible, trustworthy young adults who can make good choices when
you are not there to guide them. Follow your instincts as
to what responsibilities your child can handle and when. If
you refrain from babying them and always making things
comfortable, you will build their ability to cope when situations do not go their way.

Give them freedom and responsibility as it is earned and
warranted. If you go slow, giving them a little at a time, by
the time they leave home, they will have a sense of right
and wrong and be able to handle whatever obstacle life
sends their way. Before you know it, your quarterback will
be calling an audible and throwing a touchdown pass!

Chapter 9

...

SHOW YOUR SPIRIT

U p until now, the focus has been to help you parent like a coach. But sometimes you have to trade in your whistle for a set of pom-poms. Whether it's sports, performing arts, or any other activity where your kids have to perform or compete under pressure, coaching them from the sidelines is not helpful and can actually be harmful. According to a poll from the National Alliance for Youth Sports, about 70 percent of kids in the United States stop playing organized sports by the age of thirteen because "it's just not fun anymore."

Do you know why they say it's not fun? Because parents do not leave the coaching to the coaches. They yell instructions during the game, pull their kids aside during halftime to tell them what they should be doing, argue with coaches or program directors, question judges, and fight with other parents. While we all love our kids, the reality is most high school athletes and performers will not go on to professional sports, Broadway, or the Olympics. Yet, we behave as if their entire future is at stake. A poll from NPR, the Robert Wood Johnson Foundation, and the Harvard T. H. Chan School of Public Health cites that 26 percent of US parents of high school children who play sports hope that their child will become a professional athlete one day.

First off, one in four kids is not going to be a professional athlete. So, acting as if every game is going to make or break your child's career puts unnecessary pressure on them. The coach parent knows this and uses sports and performing as a way to teach kids all the great life lessons that can be learned from healthy competition.

The high school years are when kids need sports and the performing arts the most. They provide teens with an outlet for self-expression and pent-up aggression. These activities get them involved in structured, supervised pursuits that occupy their time and keep them out of trouble. As an added benefit, when kids are going to rehearsals and practices, they have less time to engage in the distractions of social media.

If your teen is thinking about quitting something they have always loved, make sure you are not the reason.

Don't Discredit the Authority Figure

The coach parent knows when to step back and be a spectator. The coach of a team or the director of a play is an authority figure whom your child needs to respect in order to participate. If you are constantly bad-mouthing the coach or the director to your kids, it can affect your children's attitudes, which may result in them getting less time to be featured. You also need to take the point of view of the coach or the director: How can they do their job if parents are undermining or discrediting them?

Garland Allen, a former high school athletic director, said,

> "Kids often view their coaches in a more positive light than the kid's parents. When the parent tells their kids everything the coach is doing wrong, kids tend to worry about what coach is doing incorrectly instead of following instructions."

There is great value in learning to follow instructions, even when you may not like or agree with the coach. Troy Aikman's teenage daughters play team sports at school. I asked him if, as a professional athlete, he gets involved in the coaching of his girls.

> "I let the coach coach. If my daughters were to have poor coaching, those are moments for them to work through. I'm always very supportive of the coaches, and whether I think the coach is qualified or not, I tell my daughters they have to respect the coach. The lessons you learn through sports will be present in the workplace. There is a chain of command and you have to respect that."

If a Super Bowl–winning, Hall of Fame quarterback can let someone else coach his kids without interfering, surely the coach parent can do the same.

When a parent discredits an authority figure, it sends a message that their child *does not* have to listen to this person, when in fact, in order to participate, the child *does* need to listen. In life, there will be bosses your children disagree with, and work they do not want to do, but if they want to keep their job, they will need to learn to respect authority and follow directions. When you undermine the coach, your child misses out on that important life lesson.

Coach Confidence

When I was a child, I loved to act. I even did it professionally in TV and film. Whenever I had an audition, whether for a school play or a national commercial, if my mom felt I knew my lines, then I believed I knew my lines. If I had a vocabulary test in school, and she told me I knew the words, I had the confidence to go in and ace the test. To this day, before I embark on a new project, I still call my mom to see if she thinks I can do it. When she believes I can do something, it gives me the confidence to go forward. That is the role of the coach parent. On game day or the day of the performance, you pump them up, tell them they are going to do great, and cheer them on.

Confidence Coaching

1. Boost them up.

Say something like, "You got this." "You worked hard, and you are going to be great!" "Relax and have fun. I know you can do it."

2. Avoid last-minute pointers.

Right before a game or performance, teenagers need to relax their minds and get into the zone. Inundating them with instructions will only make them more nervous.

3. Say I love you.

Before any performance, letting your kids know you love them is just a reminder that your love is a constant—whether they win or lose.

Remember, you can't compete *for* your child. They have to do that for themselves. Coach parents are supportive and do as much as they can to make their teens confident and excited to participate.

Take Your Ego Out of It

Coach parents invest a lot of time and energy in their kids. They try to be there for every game and performance, even if it means leaving work early or not getting that much-needed "me" time. We naturally root for our kids and want to see them do well. If they have an off game or a difficult meet, however, it is all part of the learning process and nothing to be ashamed of. In every football game, one team loses. That fact does not take away anything from the talent or dedication of the athletes on that team. Garland Allen shared this:

> "For many parents, it's emotional to see their child compete. They can get caught up in it. It's more an expression of their own insecurity. These parents are embarrassed when their kids do something wrong. Parents will say, 'You embarrassed me today,' based on how the kids played—as if it was

intentional. Many kids have the burden of providing their parents with self-esteem."

Recently, I witnessed what Garland was talking about
when I saw a parent at a gymnastics meet get upset with
her daughter for making mistakes in her routine. She said,
"You know that's not how we practiced it. You always have
to go and do it your way." The little girl was devastated, and
I just wanted to tell the mom to go and try to do a back
tuck and see how well *she* does.

Game Day Is Sacred

The time finally arrives for you to go see your child perform
and execute everything they've learned after weeks of practice and hard work. I asked Coach Barry Switzer how he
instructed his players on game day.

> "I told my guys, 'I've coached you all week. Now,
> let's see what you are going to do with it.' Once,
> before a game, I walked into the locker room and
> did not say a word. I wrote on the board: 'You are
> going to run 500 yards and win the game.' I threw
> my chalk down and walked out. I set the bar and
> they did it!"

Game day is just part of the process and should be the
fun payoff after all the hard work. So, on game day, stop
coaching and start cheering!

Game Day Coach Parent Principles

- **Be positive.**

When your child is competing, let them feel your positive energy from the sidelines. Clap and cheer for them.

- **Do not backseat coach.**

Screaming instructions at your kids like "box out," "hands up," and "stick the landing" only puts added pressure on them. Let them be in the moment. It's their coach's job to tell them those things—*not* yours.

- **Avoid negativity.**

Parents often scream things at their kids on the court like "Why didn't you shoot," "You should never have missed that," or "That's not what we practiced." Put yourself in the kids' shoes. Imagine that you are presenting to a client at work, and the whole time your boss is interjecting negative comments like "I can't believe you said that" or "You are totally ruining this presentation." Would you be able to present confidently?

It's Okay to Be Emotional

Even Super Bowl–winning head coach Mike Shanahan gets emotional when he watches his son, Kyle, coaching. He said,

> "When I watch Kyle [head coach of the San Francisco 49ers], being a parent, I think it's much harder being in the stands. As a parent, you are

always rooting for your kid, and you have no
control. I am more uptight watching his game in
the stands than I ever was when I was coaching
on the sidelines."

Being emotional during a game is natural and to be
expected of any parent. You can and should cheer and clap
and yell "Great shot!" But remember, taking it to the next
level and yelling at refs, coaches, judges, or opponents' parents is completely out of line. It embarrasses your child and
makes you look like a poor sport.

Don't Be a Monday Morning Quarterback

After a game or a performance, your first instinct may
be to give your child notes. But that is not the time. If
they messed up, they know it. They are looking to you for
comfort and encouragement, especially if they were not at
their best. If you are going to say something, make sure it's
something good. Sometimes it's best not to say anything at
all. Troy Aikman talked about how his parents reacted after
his high school games.

"When I played, my parents did not try to coach
me during the game or on the car rides home, and
I really appreciated that. It was tough on my buddies [when their parents coached them during or
after a game], so I liked that my parents did not
do it. With my daughters, I have kept with that."

Playing backup coach right after a game or performance is not productive. It's neither the time nor the place to try and make improvements in your children's techniques. They don't want to hear it—especially if you are critiquing them.

Choose Your Moment

Most players or performers know exactly where they went wrong. When you point it out to them when the wound is still fresh, they may not be ready to hear it. If you really feel the need to correct them or give them a note, give them some space before giving your correction. Coach Billick told a story about the coaching style of Baltimore Orioles coach Cal Ripken Sr.

> "[Former Baltimore Orioles shortstop and third baseman] Cal Ripken talked about how his dad [Cal Ripken Sr.] always had a note card. When a player made a mistake, he didn't approach them then. He would wait until the next day to come back around because he knew that, emotionally, the player was not ready to be receptive. Find the right time for the player or the child when they can be emotionally receptive. Otherwise, they are not going to hear it."

The goal of the coach parent is to be supportive and helpful. To properly effect change, resist the urge to give criticism when your kids are unable to hear or appreciate it. Waiting until the time is right will yield better results.

Someone Has to Lose

When your teen competes, there will always be times when they lose or fall short. This is the nature of competition. If your child is engaged in a solo sport or performance, the pressure is even higher because they do not have the moral support of a team. It's all on them.

When they lose, or don't score as high as they hoped, make a mistake, or forget a line, the coach parent is there to help them through it. Kim Stiefel, gymnastics coach and director of Palm Beach Gymnastics, provided some helpful tips for parents when their child does not win.

> "When a child falls short of their own expectations, whether it be disappointment, frustration, or anger, they have trouble understanding their feelings and emotions. That's the time when mom or dad needs to ground them in reality. We are not victims. We are not going to say anything to the judges or coaches. You have to lose to learn how to win, and you have to learn how to be a good loser.
>
> "It is not about that one performance or competition that creates the athlete, but a series of trials and errors and how we choose to respond to our failures and use them to our advantage in the future. Sometimes, you will not reap what you have put into the effort, but you can learn from your mistakes. It's not necessarily about going to the Olympics. Life is the Olympics."

According to Coach Stiefel, when your child loses or fails, how you behave as a coach parent can keep your kids feeling confident and strong. Here are some ideas based on her recommendations.

Give them space. After a loss or underperforming, give them a chance to process what happened.

Let them take the lead. Wait for them to speak first and let them initiate the conversation.

Point out what they did well. Coach Stiefel described an ice skater who fell repeatedly during a competition. Her mother said, "I'm proud you fell seven times, and you didn't quit or run off the ice. You finished the program, you curtsied to the judges, and finished like a polished competitor."

Do not tell them they fell short. They know how they did. There is no need to remind them or put them down for it.

Help them learn from their mistakes. A failure can be the result of not working as hard as was necessary. It's their coach's job to tell them that and your job to help them learn from the coach's feedback.

Don't blame judges, refs, or teammates for poor performance or a loss. Some of the greatest actors have opened on Broadway to terrible reviews. It doesn't mean the critiques are biased nor that they are terrible actors. Although judging is subjective, it's part of competition. If the takeaway is, *the judges just don't like me*, rather than, *maybe I need to do better,* you are robbing your child of the full benefit of the competitive experience.

Play Fair

There are no shortcuts in the game of football—nor are there in life. The coach parent always emphasizes being competitive within the standards of good conduct. Coach Jim Harbaugh highlighted what he teaches his kids and his players.

> "The thrill of competition and the best part of competition is fair, healthy, honest competition. That's how to achieve the most satisfaction. You never lie, you never cheat, and you never steal. There is an unfair advantage that can be gained every day on the field, off the field, and in life, but you must instill in your players and show them that no matter what gain was attained by cheating, it is going to be found out at some point, and the game will be undermined. That's the first and foremost lesson of sportsmanship."

Performing and competing are important parts of growing up. Often, kids learn more from the process of competing than from actually winning the game. What sticks with you for life is the discipline, the sacrifice, and the friendships that made the experience special. Tiki Barber reflected on his experience playing sports:

> "There is a camaraderie and a sense of belonging that accompanies being part of a team. It's hard to find it in life. Football is like fifty or sixty guys who have the same goal. Once you get a taste of that, it's compelling. That's how I raise my kids.

Sports are a family. It's all about being together and working toward a common goal. "

That is the experience we want our children to get from sports, performing arts, or any other activity they choose. A win is simply one possible outcome of hard work and a bit of good luck, but remember, it is fleeting. It's the experience, the life lessons, the sacrifice, and the teamwork that will stay with your children for the rest of their lives.

Chapter 10

...

THE END ZONE

Y ou've put in the hard work, made the halftime adjustments, and even coached your teens through those
personal fouls. You have fine-tuned your communication
skills, brought more structure into your home, and held
your ground through some tough battles with your teenagers. But, there is still one last play to make before you can
declare victory—building your child's character.

Teenagers are all about *them*. Add to that the "selfie" culture, and it's no wonder we have a "me" generation, where
kids believe the world cares about what they ate for break-
fast. While it's normal for teenagers to be self-involved, the
coach parent is looking to raise a young woman or man
with a strong moral compass who, when faced with ethical
dilemmas, knows exactly what to do.

Home Is Where the Heart Is

No player wants to be in the huddle with a player they can't
count on. That's why strong character is a value coaches
look for when building their team. Coach Switzer feels
character building has to start with mom and dad.

"People will say team sports build character. But just because you participate, it doesn't mean you learn right from wrong. The game teaches you self-discipline, sacrifice, and teamwork. It opens your eyes and maybe separates you from your peers because you paid a price and gave so much effort. If you are an athlete, you just do those things. But, that is not the same as having character. Character is about doing the right thing and knowing right from wrong—and that comes from the home."

Coach parents use every opportunity to teach good values, morality, and what it means to do the right thing by imparting a strong set of values to their children.

Coach Parent Values

Show gratitude.

Remember when they were little and you taught your children to say *please* and *thank you*? As they get older, take that lesson to the next step and teach them gratitude. Model and teach them simple gestures like saying thank you to the bus driver when they get off the bus. Write a thank-you note when someone has shown them kindness. When a friend likes a post, like the friend's too and be supportive of what they do.

Practice honesty.

If you are grocery shopping with your kids, and the cashier gives you too much change, make it right by giving the dollar back. If you are given credit for something done by another, give credit where it is due. If you are parking and hit another car, leaving a dent, do not pull away hoping no one will notice. Leave a note with your email so you can take care of the damage you caused. Your kids learn their behavior from you. If you cheat or are dishonest, it tells them they can be too.

Be helpful.
When you are with your son or daughter and you see someone in need of help, instruct your children to get involved. One day, my son and I had just come out of our building on an icy day, and we saw an elderly man slip and fall. Rather than just walking by, we helped him up and stayed with him until the ambulance arrived. Another time, my daughter and I saw a little girl wandering in a department store. We were in a rush, but we stopped and stayed with her until we were able to reunite her with her mother.

Be courteous.
While it may seem old-fashioned, raising your son to be a gentleman and your daughter to be a lady is a trait that can go a long way. Teach your kids to let older people out of an elevator first; give up a seat on the bus or train to the elderly or a pregnant woman; avoid texting when someone is speaking to you; cover your mouth when you yawn; excuse yourself when you need to pass gas or burp; refrain from cursing in public; and shake hands with a firm handshake and make eye contact when you greet someone.

Be caring.
Dartmouth's Coach Buddy Teevens says, "I teach my team that when they get a new teammate or a coach or meet new people in life, they must always remember the acronym CARE:

Continued

Consider: We don't all come from the same background. Think about why someone feels as they do and try to understand it.

Accept: You may not have the same opinions and that is okay.

Respect: Respect everybody, no matter their position in life.

Educate: Educate yourself, which means 'If you don't know, ask.'"

Share Your Trophy

Teens like to complain, saying things like "My life sucks. My parents suck. The world sucks . . . " You get my point. It's the coach parent's job to show their teen how much their life does *not* suck. Coach Coughlin related how he inspired both his players and his children to be community-minded.

"I have found over the years that players are very good with kids, and they are good with people who are less fortunate than they are. At the New York Giants, if there was ever a Make-a-Wish child who wanted to come, they were invited with open arms. I would say hello and tell the kids to prepare a message for the team for when they are in the huddle with the players. The kids would get nervous and stop thinking of themselves as they would make their speech, and the players would cheer for them. The guys who were their favorite players would take pictures with them and their family. The players did not know the kids, but they understood the purpose and the importance of being part of something bigger than themselves."

Every coach and player I spoke with was involved in charitable causes and many, like Coach Coughlin, have started their own charities. While your teenagers do not have the resources of an entire football team, they can still make a difference. There are so many ways to give back. For teenagers, it's important they get personally involved. Whether it's building a house, feeding the homeless, picking up trash, mentoring, or organizing clothing drives, the key is to make it meaningful for them.

No matter where you live, find ways to participate in community service with your kids. If you see a problem in your community, think of ways your family can help.

Here are a few ideas to get started.

1. Sign up for walks and runs with your kids to support a cause in your community.

2. Have a bake sale or car wash in front of your home to raise money for a cause that is meaningful to your children.

3. Feed the homeless together at a local soup kitchen.

4. Go to www.dosomething.org. They have several campaigns where teenagers can join other teenagers in community-service projects such as sports equipment drives, cleaning parks, and preventing texting and driving.

Find Your Faith

Many football locker rooms hold prayer circles before a big game. It's common for teams to have a chaplain for players to talk to when they need guidance. In my research, I found faith to play a major role in the lives of many of the coaches and players I interviewed. I was curious to know what role faith played in football and whether faith could be helpful to the coach parent.

Teenagers do not always know how to understand the difficulties that happen in life, and faith can be a way to help them through a hard time. It can also give them hope and focus their energy toward something bigger than themselves.

Since many teams pray before a game, I asked Coach John Harbaugh what the players and coaches prayed for.

> "We pray to stay healthy, pray to put our best foot forward—whatever is in our hearts. It's okay to pray to win, too."

Even if faith is not a part of your life, exposing your children to it can be something they find useful. They can choose to believe or not to believe in God, but there is a lot to learn from faith. Faith-based groups are, by their very nature, grounded in ethics and morality. If you send your teenager to a weekly religious program or youth group, they will have a place to learn to handle ethical dilemmas, socialize in a supervised setting, and engage in community-building activities.

Community Service

When I wanted my children to find community-service projects, I found the faith-based groups had the most organized and well-supervised programs. My son went with his youth group to New Orleans to help residents who were still suffering from the aftermath of Hurricane Katrina. They planted gardens of food, visited local churches and synagogues, and learned firsthand about the devastation the people had suffered.

My daughter loves to sing and enjoyed being part of her choir and performing at senior homes. Last year, my son went to Selma, Alabama, with his youth group on a civil rights trip and learned about the sacrifices and injustices people faced during the civil rights movement years. Because we have been involved in our faith-based community since our kids were little, they are excited to participate in these trips because they go with all their friends. The parents have each other's emails, so we connect when there is a midnight run to feed the homeless or a community outreach project, to assure our kids that all their friends will be there too.

Seek Guidance

Unlike a therapist, a chaplain can give advice and help your child make a decision that is ethical and moral—not just one that feels good to them in the moment. While you may not realize it, there may be issues in your home that your teenagers don't feel comfortable discussing with you or a family member. If your teens can turn to and connect with someone of faith for guidance, it is one more layer of support to keep them on the right path. When Coach Wannstedt coached, he always wanted his players to have someone they could talk to:

> "Every team has a chapel service before the game. I brought in my own chaplain, who was at every practice. I believed that having someone from a faith-based perspective that the players could get to know and trust and communicate with was important—and the players would attest to that. And it wasn't necessarily conversation about religion. Maybe they needed to talk about a girlfriend or a teammate. I created a situation that was another avenue for the players to go for support."

Sportsmanship

My friend's eleven-year-old daughter is an ice-skater. While she may not be of Olympic caliber, she can hold her own. She was asked to compete in a statewide competition and had a beautiful red skating dress for the event.

The mother of a set of twins who were also competing told her daughters to hide the red skating costume in their locker, forcing my friend's daughter to wear something else at the last minute. The plan worked. My friend's daughter was distracted and didn't skate to the best of her ability. The twins placed higher than my friend's child and learned that cheating could get them ahead.

For the next competition, the twins didn't practice as hard as they should have. Instead, they went and hid my friend's daughter's pink sparkly bows. By that time, however, my friend was on to them and had left "decoy" bows for them to take instead of the real ones. The twins placed last. Their mother was furious and claimed the judges were in the wrong.

Encouraging your kids to throw an elbow when the ref is not looking or to hide a girl's tutu before a performance is behavior that should never be suggested or encouraged, no matter how competitive a parent might be.

Regarding parents who encourage their kids to cheat or play dirty to get ahead, Coach Wannstedt said something we should all keep in mind:

> "You can cut corners, and it might work out one time, but you can't do it your whole career."

Even if your kids are the next superstar athletes, they won't make it very far if they get ahead by cheating. Coach Zimmer explained how he coaches sportsmanship:

> "We talk about our work ethic and doing things right. We have a saying: outwork, outrun, and outhit. We try to play the game the right way. We

abide by the rules. We don't coach penalties. I want them to respect the game and the way we play."

Troy Aikman added,

"When I tell my girls to show good sportsmanship, it means they will be respectful to the opponent, help them up, not talk trash, and be a great competitor—but always be courteous."

As competitive as professional football is, the coaches and the players value sportsmanship and fair play. Remember, if people are cheating, there is no glory in the win.

Respect Your Opponent

A worthy opponent makes you a better player and provides you with the opportunity to play the game you love. Of course, you should want to destroy the competition during the game. But once the clock has run out, everyone must show respect for one another. Coach Mariucci gave an example:

"Watch college basketball. Every player and coach shakes hands with every player and coach on the opposing team every game—win, lose, or draw. It's called sportsmanship. It's called respect for the game. That's the way it should be. If I were to ever see my kids or my players show poor sportsmanship, I would be all over it. The kids and the players grow up respecting the game, the opponent, and how things are done properly."

Coach Parent Principles of Sportsmanship

No cheating.
Never encourage your children to cheat at anything, and reprimand cheating if you see it—even if no one else catches them.

Adhere to the rules.
When children compete, whether it is in school, on the field, the stage, or in life, encourage them to learn and follow rules.

Be a sport.
Always shake hands with your opponent after a game and say something complimentary. It doesn't hurt you to say something nice to someone else.

Be gracious.
Both parents and their kids should thank all the volunteers that made the game or performance possible.

Be respectful.
Always be mindful of the time and effort people have put in. You may not like a ref's call, but they are spending their Saturday refereeing your child's game, so you and your children should treat them with respect.

Winning Behavior

When football players are true winners, they treat the custodial staff with the same respect as the head coach. They smile and say hello to everyone, and they stop to give a kid an autograph. They go to a hospital to make a fan's day.

They go out of their way to give back to their community. Coach Switzer expressed this concept effectively:

> "We define ourselves by how we treat others and behave in the presence of others. Sometimes, we only have a matter of minutes and seconds to leave a lasting impression. You can be crude, rude, arrogant, or obstinate. But it doesn't cost you a thing to be nice. Nice is a better choice. The rewards can be unimaginable, and you will never know when being nice will come back to you."

When I started on this journey to define coach parenting, I wondered if the coaches and players I interviewed would be larger than life and not have time or want to take a real interest in talking to me about coaching—let alone parenting. When I began each interview, I was a little nervous and probably had a bit of a quiver in my voice. After all, these guys are legends!

But, in *every* case, they immediately put me at ease. They were kind, patient, and made me feel like I was the most important person they had to talk to all day. They *wanted* to share their knowledge and wisdom. Coach John Harbaugh even thanked me for calling him and told me how much he loved the idea of coach parenting. It was like I was one of his players, and he was giving me that pregame talk that made me feel invincible. Coach Mariucci sent me a film called *Father Figures* that he did with NFL Films when his kids were little, where he discussed the similarities of coaching and being a dad.

Coach Billick put it most succinctly:

> "Whether it's the firm hand of a Tom Coughlin or
> the communicative style of a Pete Carroll [Seattle
> Seahawks head coach], all these coaches are great
> teachers and communicators."

I hope I have communicated to you the insight these brilliant coaches and players shared with me. Hopefully, you learned a little about coaching football along the way too. I know I did. You have studied your coach parenting playbook. Now, it's time to go back into your locker room, rally your players, and lead them to the field to play their best game ever!

THE COACHES, PLAYERS, AND CONTRIBUTORS

Troy Aikman

Fox lead NFL analyst and former Dallas Cowboys quarterback Troy Aikman's playing career included setting forty-five Dallas Cowboys passing records. When he led one of sports' most famous franchises, the Cowboys won six NFC East titles (1992–96 and 1998) and advanced to four NFC Championship Games (1992–95). Aikman is one of only four quarterbacks to guide his team to victory in three Super Bowls (XXVII, XXVIII, and XXX). In 2006, Aikman was voted into the Pro Football Hall of Fame in Canton, Ohio.

Garland Allen

A retired high school teacher, coach, and athletic director, Allen is currently on the faculty at New York University's Institute for Sports Management, Media, and Business. He has lectured extensively on building healthy young athletes, and on defining the appropriate role of parents in youth sports. He has coached football, basketball, and track and field. Allen is a graduate of Kent State and Fairfield Universities.

Tiki Barber

Barber graduated from the University of Virginia's McIntire School of Commerce (Phi Eta Sigma honor society). At UVA, he excelled both academically and athletically—in both football and track and field. During his ten-year NFL career with the New York Giants, Barber became one of three NFL players in football history with at least 10,000 yards rushing and 5,000 yards receiving. He holds almost every Giants rushing record—total yards, rushing yards, rushing attempts—and is second in rushing touchdowns. He currently co-hosts CBS Sports Radio's *Tiki and Tierney* program.

Brian Billick

Billick spent seven seasons (1992–98) as the offensive coordinator for the Minnesota Vikings under then head coach Dennis Green. In 1999, he became head coach of the Baltimore Ravens, where he remained until 2007. In his second season with Baltimore, the franchise won its first championship, at Super Bowl XXXV, with a 34–7 victory over the New York Giants. Billick is now an NFL Network analyst appearing on *NFL GameDay First* and *NFL Total Access*.

Bob Costas

While attending Syracuse University, Costas began his professional career at WSYR-TV and radio in 1973, before joining KMOX radio in St. Louis in 1974. He has been with NBC since 1980 and has won 27 Emmy awards—more than any sports broadcaster. His peers have named him "National Sportscaster of the Year" a record eight times, and in 2012 he was elected to the National Sportscasters and Sportswriters Hall of Fame. From baseball's "Game of the Week" in the 1980s through his hosting of the Olympics, the late-night program *Later with Bob Costas*, his programs on HBO, and eight Super Bowl broadcasts, Costas has been a prominent part of the coverage of every major sport for more than three decades.

Tom Coughlin

A veteran of twenty-nine years in the NFL, including twenty-one as a head coach, Coughlin ranks as the twelfth-winningest coach in NFL history. Coughlin led the New York Giants to two Super Bowl victories against the New England Patriots, becoming the thirteenth coach in NFL history to claim multiple Super Bowl titles. He is one of only nineteen head coaches with a perfect record in Super Bowl games. Coughlin was the Jacksonville Jaguars' head coach for nine seasons and the New York Giants' for twelve. He is now the executive vice president of football operations for the Jacksonville Jaguars.

James D. Dunning Jr.

Founder of Dunning Group Inc., a private company specializing in media, energy, and other leveraged investments, Dunning also has served as an officer and chairman of many public and private companies. He is a former member of the board of trustees of Deerfield Academy and the University of Pennsylvania, and is currently an overseer of athletics at the university. He is a director of TeenAIDS Peer Corps.

Jay Fiedler

Fiedler played football and ran track and field for Dartmouth College while earning a bachelor of arts degree in engineering sciences. He went on to play ten years as an NFL quarterback, where he rose from undrafted free agent to starting quarterback and captain of his team. During four years with the Miami Dolphins he had three winning seasons, an AFC East title, and two postseason appearances. He concluded his career with the New York Jets in 2005, the same year he was selected for the National Jewish Sports Hall of Fame. Fiedler is the full-time director of the Sports Academy at Brookwood Camps and also runs football clinics, camps, and events as director of Prime Time Sports Camps.

Jedd Fisch

Fisch is the offensive coordinator of the UCLA Bruins football team. He was formerly the University of Michigan Wolverines football quarterbacks coach, wide receivers coach, and passing game coordinator under Jim Harbaugh from 2015 to 2016. During more than a decade with the NFL, Fisch coached with the Baltimore Ravens, the Denver Broncos, the Seattle Seahawks, and the Jacksonville Jaguars.

Jim Harbaugh

Jim Harbaugh is a member of a renowned coaching family. He is the former head coach of the San Francisco 49ers, where he led the franchise to the NFC Championship Game in each of his first three seasons. He followed up with an appearance in Super Bowl XLVII in 2012. Harbaugh's 49ers lost a back-and-forth affair, 34–31, to the Baltimore Ravens and his brother, John, in one of the most dramatic games—and the only matchup of brothers as head coaches—in NFL history. He helped guide San Francisco back to the NFC title game in 2013. He is now the head coach of the University of Michigan Wolverines football team.

John Harbaugh

Super Bowl–winning head coach John Harbaugh has led the Baltimore Ravens to a playoff berth in six (2008–12 and 2014) of his nine seasons in Baltimore, and in 2012 his team captured the franchise's second world championship, in Super Bowl XLVII. John and his younger brother, Jim, the former 49ers head coach, are the only NFL head coaches to reach three conference championships in the first five seasons of a coaching career.

Jimmy Johnson

Johnson was the first to coach teams to both a collegiate championship (University of Miami in 1987) and a Super Bowl championship. As head coach of the Dallas Cowboys from 1989 to 1994, he was the architect of the team's consecutive victories in Super Bowls XXVII and XXVIII. When he retired from the Cowboys he joined Fox Sports, only to return to a head coaching position in 1996 with the Miami Dolphins for four years. He resumed his broadcasting role in 2002 with Fox Sports, where he is an NFL lead analyst.

Howie Long

A second-round draft pick out of Villanova in 1981, Long became one of the best defensive linemen ever to play in the NFL. His size, strength, and quickness, combined with his versatility (he played all five defensive line positions), helped define his era. Long played in eight Pro Bowls and was twice named the NFL's Lineman of the Year by the NFL Alumni Association. In 1983, Long's Oakland Raiders prevailed in Super Bowl XVIII against the Washington Redskins. Long was selected as one of two defensive ends on the 1980s All-Decade Team. He was inducted into the Pro Football Hall of Fame in 2000 and is a Fox lead NFL analyst.

Steve Mariucci

Mariucci's coaching journey began in 1978 at his alma mater, Northern Michigan, as the quarterbacks and running backs coach. In 1992, he joined Mike Holmgren's coaching staff with the Green Bay Packers as quarterbacks coach, where he helped mold the talents of future Hall of Famer Brett Favre. He was an NFL head coach for nine years, spending six with the San Francisco 49ers and three with the Detroit Lions. He led the 49ers to four playoff appearances, including a trip to the NFC Championship Game in 1997, and he holds the NFL record for most consecutive regular season wins at home to begin a coaching career (18). He currently is an analyst on the NFL Network.

Mike Shanahan

From 1995 to 2008, Shanahan was the head coach of the Denver Broncos. He led the franchise to its first Super Bowl title, in 1997, and to a consecutive Super Bowl victory in

1998. He also served as the head coach of the Los Angeles Raiders and Washington Redskins. Over the course of his long career, Shanahan has coached in eight college bowl games, two NCAA national championships, ten NFL conference championships, and six Super Bowls.

Kim Stiefel

Kim Stiefel has been actively involved in the sport of gymnastics since 1976 as a competitor, coach, judge, and National Instructor for USA Gymnastics, educating instructors to facilitate superior coaching techniques. She holds a bachelor of science degree in physical education and is the mother of a competitive figure skater.

Barry Switzer

Switzer served for sixteen years as head football coach at the University of Oklahoma and four years as head coach for the NFL's Dallas Cowboys, during which time the Cowboys won Super Bowl XXX. He has one of the highest winning percentages of any college football coach in history, and is one of only three head coaches to win both a college football national championship and a Super Bowl.

Eugene F. (Buddy) Teevens III

Teevens, who as a player led Dartmouth to the 1978 Ivy League championship and as a coach led Dartmouth football to back-to-back Ivy League titles in 1990 and 1991, returned as the head coach of the Big Green football program in 2005 and won another title in 2015. Teevens has been an integral part of the Manning Passing Academy since its inception, and as an associate director he oversees all aspects of the on-field operation and coaching staff. He also has appeared on panels for "Practice Like Pros" to extol the virtues of reducing full-contact practices by focusing on technique, to limit injuries. Teevens is currently the head coach of the Dartmouth Big Green football team.

Kenneth Tinsley

At Central State University in Ohio, Tinsley played tight end and with special teams, and graduated cum laude in 2013 with a degree in business administration. He started his coaching career at Eastern Senior High School in his hometown of Washington, D.C., where he was the assistant offensive coordinator and wide receivers coach. He became the wide receivers coach and special teams assistant at Bates College, and spent the 2016–17 season on the staff at Morrisville State College in New York as a wide receivers coach.

Lawrence Tynes

Tynes played four seasons with the Kansas City Chiefs and was traded to the New York Giants in 2007. In his first season with the Giants, he kicked the game-winning field goal in overtime against the Green Bay Packers in the NFC Championship Game, which qualified the Giants for Super Bowl XLII. He kicked another overtime field goal against the San Francisco 49ers in the 2011–12 NFC Championship Game, which qualified the Giants for Super Bowl XLVI. He won two Super Bowl rings with the Giants in 2007 and 2011. Tynes is the only player in NFL history to have two overtime game-winning field goals in the playoffs.

Mark Unterberg

Mark Unterberg, M.D., F.A.P.A., F.A.C.Psa, is a clinical professor of psychiatry at the University of Texas Southwestern Medical School. He is board certified in Adult Psychiatry and was board certified in Addiction Psychiatry (added qualifications 1994–2004). Dr. Unterberg is currently the WWE's chief psychiatrist and consultant for WWE's wellness program. Dr. Unterberg was the team psychiatrist for the Dallas Cowboys for thirty years (1979–2009) and is an NFL clinician for the NFL Players' Program of Substance Abuse. He was also the team psychiatrist for both the Texas Rangers and the Dallas Mavericks.

Dick Vermeil

Vermeil's tenure as a head coach began with the Philadelphia Eagles for seven seasons starting in 1976. Vermeil led the team to four playoff appearances, an NFC Championship win, and a trip to Super Bowl XV in 1980. After leaving the Eagles, Vermeil began a fourteen-year broadcasting career as an NFL and college football analyst for CBS and ABC. In 1997, Vermeil returned to the NFL as head coach of the St. Louis Rams and led the team to its first Super Bowl victory. In 2001, Vermeil became the head coach of the Kansas City Chiefs. Following his fifth season with the Chiefs, Vermeil retired, leaving as the team's third-winningest coach.

Dave Wannstedt

In 1989, Wannstedt was named defensive coordinator of the Dallas Cowboys, and in 1992 the squad won Super Bowl XXVII. From there, he became head coach of the

Chicago Bears for six seasons. In 2000, Wannstedt was named head coach of the Miami Dolphins, posting a 41–23 record over the next four seasons, including playoff berths in 2000 and 2001. In 2005, Wannstedt went back to his alma mater, the University of Pittsburgh, and served as head coach for six years. In 2010, he returned to the NFL, serving on the staff for the Buffalo Bills (2011–12) and Tampa Bay Buccaneers (2013). He is now a Fox Sports NFL and college football studio analyst.

Charlie Williams

Williams has coached football for more than three decades. He spent six seasons (1996–2001) as receivers coach for the Tampa Bay Buccaneers under head coach Tony Dungy. His years coaching college players included a season for Lou Holtz at South Carolina in 2003 and multiyear tenures as a wide receivers coach at the University of Arizona and the University of North Carolina, between 2004 and 2011. He served as the Indianapolis Colts' receivers coach from 2012 to 2015. Currently, he is the University of South Florida Bulls' wide receivers coach.

Mike Zimmer

Zimmer is entering his fourth season as the head coach of the Minnesota Vikings in 2017. In his second season leading the Vikings in 2015, Zimmer piloted the club to an NFC North title and a Wild Card Playoff berth. In his NFL tenure, Zimmer has been a part of twelve playoff teams and teams that have won eight division titles. He coached the Cowboys defensive backs when Dallas won Super Bowl XXX after the 1995 season. Coaching is a

Zimmer family tradition. His son Adam is coaching the Vikings linebackers and his father, Bill, was inducted into the Illinois High School Football Coaches Association Hall of Fame.

ABOUT THE AUTHOR

 Erika Katz is the author of the *Bonding Over Beauty* parenting book series that teaches mothers how to bond with their tween daughters. The series focuses on encouraging and strengthening the mother–daughter relationship and helps mothers navigate sensitive topics that often arise with tween daughters.

Erika is regularly featured as a parenting expert guest of *The Today Show*, *Access Hollywood*, *Access Hollywood Live*, *Fox News*, *Inside Edition*, *The Doctors*, *The Meredith Vieira Show*, *NBC News 4 New York*, *Fox 5 New York*, *CBS2 New York*, *PIX11 News*, and Telemundo. She discusses parenting, social media, beauty, lifestyle, and how to keep children safe. She also contributes her expertise to the *New York Post*, *Seventeen*, *Parents*, *Good Housekeeping*, *Girl's Life*, *Shape*, *Prevention*, *Parenting*, and many online blogs and websites. Erika gives seminars on keeping kids safe on social media and navigating the latest apps.

As a spokesperson for Invisalign® clear aligners, Erika wrote a parenting guide for parents of middle school and high school called "Unbrace Teen Confidence." She travels all over the country for Invisalign® to promote building teen confidence.

A graduate of Dartmouth College, Erika lives in New York City with her husband and two children.

CPSIA information can be obtained
at www.ICGtesting.com
Printed in the USA
LVOW11s0109281017
554097LV00001B/68/P

DEC 0 5 2017